KU-428-941

Professor David Wilson is one of the country's leading crimin-ologists, and has written several academic books and papers on serial killers. He is the author of *A History of British Serial Killing* and co-author of *Hunting Evil: Inside the Ipswich Serial Murders* with Paul Harrison. He is the Director of the Centre for Applied Criminology at Birmingham City University.

Paul Harrison is a highly respected Sky News correspondent, where he has covered the Asian tsunami, the war in Afghani-stan and Slobodan Milosevic's trial at The Hague. He reported extensively on the Steve Wright and Peter Tobin trials.

Also by David Wilson and Paul Harrison

Hunting Evil: Inside the Ipswich Serial Murders

The Lost British Serial Killer

Closing the Case on Peter Tobin and Bible John

DAVID WILSON and
PAUL HARRISON

sphere

SPHERE

First published in Great Britain in 2010 by Sphere
Reprinted 2010, 2011 (twice), 2014

A CIP catalogue record for this book
is available from the British Library.

ISBN 978-0-7515-4232-5

Typeset in Caslon by M Rules
Printed and bound in Great Britain by
Clays Ltd, St Ives plc

Papers used by Sphere are from well-managed forests
and other responsible sources.

MIX
Paper from
responsible sources
FSC® C104740

Sphere
An imprint of
Little, Brown Book Group
100 Victoria Embankment
London EC4Y 0DY

An Hachette UK Company
www.hachette.co.uk

www.littlebrown.co.uk

Contents

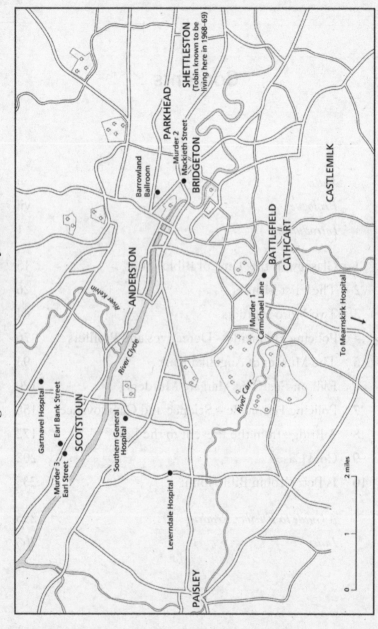

Glasgow at the time of the Bible John murders

Prologue

It was Thursday, 30 October 1969 and neither of them knew how the night would end. But that was part of the thrill. So far, the 'Over-25s' night at the Barrowland Ballroom had been worth every shilling – as it was every Thursday. Jeannie Williams and her sister Helen Puttock had both had a few drinks, and Jeannie especially had partied the night away, spending much of the evening on the dance floor.

At closing time, the two women started their long journey home. They left by the Gallowgate entrance and walked the familiar few hundred chilly yards to Glasgow Cross to hail a cab. For a while, they were accompanied by two men they had met at the dancehall. Both were called 'John', or at least that was what they claimed. Then Jeannie's John hurriedly announced that he was going to catch the last bus home and disappeared into the night. She wasn't surprised. He'd told her he was from Castlemilk, and while he'd never admitted it, she'd guessed from early on in the night that he was married. But in truth, she hadn't really concentrated on what he'd said, and nor did she care that he might have a wife waiting at home for him; she had been far too busy enjoying herself. She thought he was just a typical Glasgow punter out on the pull at the Barrowland. But he was a good dancer and they had enjoyed each other's company enough to spend most of the evening together.

Helen's John was an altogether different kettle of fish – definitely not the usual Barrowland type. For a start, he was polite, well spoken and didn't swear every second word. Jeannie thought he would have been better suited to the Albert Ballroom in Bath Street on the other side of the city, which was a much higher-quality dancehall. Her opinion had been reinforced when he'd called the Barrowland and places like it 'dens of iniquity', before adding, even more pointedly, that married women went there to look for men. He called them 'adulterous' women.

His accent was West End, but not quite posh enough to identify him as a resident of Milngavie or Kelvinside – although he did mention golf and said that his cousin had once hit a hole in one. He was tall – almost six foot – aged between twenty-five and thirty-five, and had a distinctive missing tooth as well as slightly overlapping front teeth. Jeannie had noticed his teeth earlier because her eye line had been at the same level as his mouth. His sandy hair was cut short and rounded at the back, which was very unusual at the time in Glasgow, where long hair was all the rage. His smartness extended to what he was wearing, too: short suede boots, a brown suit with three buttons on the front, a blue shirt, and a dark tie with three red stripes across it. Jeannie wondered if it might have been a regimental or even an old school tie.

Jeannie, Helen and the one remaining John caught a cab and soon it was travelling along Argyle Street. By then, Jeannie was thinking that this John wanted to see the back of her so he could be alone with Helen. That would have to wait, though, because the two sisters lived close to each other in the west of the city. The driver headed up the Dumbarton Road, through Partick, and on towards their homes in Scotstoun.

After a while, John reached into his inside pocket and pulled out a packet of Embassy cigarettes. Then he gallantly offered one to Helen. Jeannie couldn't remember him offering anyone a cigarette during the whole evening at the Barrowland, so she was surprised by this act of generosity. Before he had a chance to put the packet back in his pocket, she asked for one for herself. He seemed distracted, so she took the opportunity to grab three.

Although Jeannie continued to chat amiably with Helen, she grew increasingly uneasy about John's attitude. She remembered him saying his surname was something like Templeton or Sempleson or Emerson, but she hadn't caught it properly and it hadn't cropped up again. That was hardly surprising as he barely attempted to make conversation, although he did mention that he worked in a laboratory and went drinking in Yoker, a mile up the Dumbarton Road from Scotstoun.

'But I don't drink at Hogmanay. I pray,' he insisted.

Jeannie thought the comment was strange, especially as when the rivalry between Rangers and Celtic football clubs had come up in conversation, John had said he 'couldn't be bothered with all that religious carry on'. Even stranger was that he seemed to know something about the Bible, and talked about foster children and a woman who had been stoned to death. He hadn't quoted Scripture directly, but Jeannie thought she recognised what he was saying as a story from the Old

Testament. She found him aloof and broody, and arrogant in the way he would avoid answering a direct question. She had seen this side of his personality earlier at the Barrowland – after some money had got stuck in the cigarette machine. John had demanded to see the manager and had given him and the bouncers a piece of his mind.

In total, the journey took about twenty minutes. The taxi pulled over in Kelso Street, Scotstoun. By rights, Helen and John should have got out first, as Jeannie's house was a little further on than Helen's, which was in Earl Street. But John insisted that Jeannie should be dropped off first, rather than leave her alone with the taxi driver. The cab could then double back to Helen's. Jeannie wondered if he was simply trying to be chivalrous again.

'Goodnight,' Jeannie shouted as she closed the taxi's door. 'I'll maybe see you next week.' As the taxi sped off, she was worried about how keen John had been to get her out of the cab. But she contented herself with the thought that it wouldn't be long before Helen was safe at home. Or so Jeannie thought.

At about 2 a.m., a night bus picked up a dishevelled man who had earlier been seen walking up Dumbarton Road, which ran parallel to Earl Street. Some of the passengers noticed that he wore a dirty jacket and had a bruise on his cheek. He eventually got off the bus at the junction of Dumbarton Road and Gray Street.

The following morning, Archie MacIntyre was walking his black Labrador behind the blocks of flats along Earl Street at 7.25 a.m. He saw a woman lying next to a drainpipe, half un-dressed, but still wearing her fake-fur coat. Helen Puttock had not made it home safely. John's apparent chivalry had masked an evil intent.

Until the moment when the taxi had pulled up near to Helen's home on Earl Street the previous night and the taxi driver had been paid and dismissed, all might have seemed fine to Helen. But the police reasoned that the situation had then rapidly got out of hand. First there had been a kiss, then a fierce struggle. At one point Helen had tried to run away, scrambling up the grass verge of a railway line that ran parallel to Earl Street. But John had obviously caught her, then punched and beat her around her head, knocking her unconscious. Next he had dragged her back to where he would kill her – perhaps because it would be out of sight of passers-by. Turning her over and kneeling on her, almost as if he were praying, he had taken one of Helen's stockings and used it to squeeze the life out of her. He had then tucked her sanitary towel neatly under her armpit.

Naturally, the police turned first to Jeannie in their bid to identify Helen's killer, and she was desperate to remember every last thing about him. Over the months and years to come, Jeannie replayed in her mind every second of that Thursday night and the taxi ride across Glasgow. Could something have slipped her memory? Perhaps some tiny, seemingly insignificant detail might provide a clue; a key piece to complete the jigsaw puzzle. She knew that the story she told and the description she provided could be absolutely vital to the police investigation.

With Helen's death, the Glasgow Police realised they were hunting what we would now call a 'serial killer' – one who preyed on women in Glasgow's dancehalls. Over the previous twenty months, two other women – Patricia Docker and Jemima McDonald – had also been murdered after nights out at the Barrowland. The police were convinced that the three murders were the work of one man. Due to the religious nature of his conversations, he became known as 'Bible John'.

Jeannie eventually agreed to be hypnotised to try to remember as much as possible about the man. But by then she had already recalled a great deal and had told the police everything she knew. Jeannie and the police were convinced that Helen's killer would soon be identified and arrested. No one thought it would be forty years before such evil showed itself in Glasgow again.

Introduction

Policing the Commuting Serial Killer

> The fact that Sutcliffe managed to evade capture for
> five years was not due to his intelligence but rather to
> an astounding lack of it on the part of the police. Had
> the killer left a photograph of himself, posing with a
> foot on each victim, English police chiefs of such out-
> standing quality might have caught him eventually.
>
> Ian Brady, *The Gates of Janus: Serial Killing
> and Its Analysis* (2001)

Whisper it quietly, but one reason why serial killers often
evade detection for many years is that our police are not very
good at catching them. Forget what you've read in books or
seen at the cinema, where the detective finally but inevitably
'gets his man'. The reality is that serial killers who are mobile
and organised – 'commuters' who cross from one police force
area in one part of the country into another while carefully covering their tracks – can stay ahead of the police for decades.
Often it's simply a matter of luck, rather than brilliant detective work, that brings a killer to justice.

For the police investigating the murders of Patricia Docker, Jemima (Mima) McDonald and Helen Puttock, there was a distinct lack of such luck for many years. Furthermore, certainly at first, there was little to suggest that Bible John was a commuting serial killer. The three victims were murdered by the same man in a twenty-month period between 1968 and 1969 in one city, Glasgow. He even picked up all three at the same place: the Barrowland Ballroom.

The police also had some evidence and plenty of witnesses. A number of people had seen the handsome, well-dressed, personable, Bible-quoting young man who picked up the women – before he abused and strangled them. There was also the tantalising possibility that a semen stain which he left on Helen Puttock's stocking might eventually produce a DNA profile. Forensic science was in its infancy in the 1960s, but even back then scientists were well aware of its potential as a tool in the fight against serious crime. They just needed to develop their techniques for utilising it.

As the 1970s approached, the investigation into the Bible John murders remained a top priority, but the police's leads seemed to be going nowhere. Obviously there was deep concern that he would soon strike again. But after the murder of Helen Puttock, the Glasgow dancehall killings stopped. Was Bible John on the move? Had there been too much heat in Glasgow, so staying in the city had been too risky? Perhaps he had simply grown tired of killing, or had been arrested and imprisoned for other offences. Perhaps he had died. His potential victims remained as alert as ever. Talk of Bible John filled the city's dancehalls almost as much as the music, and the local police knew exactly the type of man they were looking for. But for whatever reason, as far as Glasgow was concerned, Bible John seemed to have vanished into thin air. Just as a number of other women throughout the country started to disappear, or were found murdered.

It is here that Peter Tobin enters our story. He was living in Glasgow at the same time as the first of the Bible John murders. He visited the same dancehalls as Bible John. Like Bible John, he sexually abused women whom he met at dancehalls. And, as of December 2009, had been convicted of murdering three women and so could be described as a serial killer. Just like Bible John.

Peter Britton Tobin was born on 27 August 1946 in Johnstone, Scotland. One of seven brothers and sisters, he inherited the same heart condition that would eventually kill his father in July 1979. The young Tobin also experienced the loss of a younger brother, who asphyxiated during childbirth in October 1952. A loner, often shunned and bullied by other children in his tough Clydeside neighbourhood, Tobin's anti-social behaviour seems to have landed him in an approved school by the age of seven. His teenage years were punctuated by petty crime and odd jobs to pay his way. A stint in the armed forces ended prematurely, and by nineteen he was serving a fifteen-month sentence for theft and fraud at St John's List D School in Glasgow. A couple of months after his release he was caught stealing a car, which earned him another three months in the same institution. When he next came out he started to move around the country, finding work as he went as an odd-job man. Sometimes there seemed to be little logic behind his choice of destination, but wherever Peter Tobin went, misery seemed to accompany him.

He first came to national attention in 1994, when he was convicted of raping and molesting two fourteen-year-old schoolgirls in Portsmouth. He'd moved to the south coast to be close to his estranged wife and son, and had targeted two girls who had come to see his neighbour. Tobin was sentenced to fourteen years' imprisonment, but he was released in 2004 and placed on the sex offenders register.

Soon afterwards, he returned to Glasgow, putting nearly five hundred miles between his crimes and a new stage in his life. He also adopted the pseudonym 'Pat McLaughlin'. Posing as a homeless person, he convinced a priest at St Patrick's church in Anderston to employ him as a handyman. This allowed him to avoid any unwanted attention until the arrival of a Polish student called Angelika Kluk, whom Tobin would later rape and murder. In this brutal attack, he stabbed Angelika sixteen times in the chest, then hid her body under the floorboards of the church, close to the confessional. DNA evidence ultimately played a major role in convicting Tobin of this murder, and he was sentenced to a minimum of twenty-one years in prison. The same DNA evidence also led to a history of murder dating back at least sixteen years, and started to reveal the full extent of Tobin's commuting killings.

While investigating the Kluk murder, detectives discovered – through diligence, rather than luck – something that linked Tobin with the disappearance of the schoolgirl Vicky Hamilton, who had vanished in Bathgate in 1991: Tobin had lived in the town at the time. Vicky's body was finally found many miles from Bathgate, in a shallow grave in Tobin's former back garden in Margate, Kent. In the winter of 2008 he was sentenced to thirty years at Dundee High Court for Vicky's murder.

In the course of excavating Tobin's garden, the police also discovered the body of a second young woman – Dinah McNicol – whose remains were found under the patio. Dinah, an eighteen-year-old student, had failed to return to her home in Tillingham, Essex, after hitch-hiking back from a pop festival in Hampshire the same year that Vicky had vanished.

Once the police had found irrefutable evidence that Tobin had committed murder three times, naturally they started to suspect that he might have killed other women, too. It was around this time that he started to be linked to the Glasgow dancehall murders, with many people speculating that Tobin was indeed the infamous 'Bible John'. In prison, awaiting trial for Vicky Hamilton's murder, Tobin boasted to the prison psychiatrist that he had killed forty-eight women, but he then refused to give any details to the police.

Nevertheless, there can be no doubt that Peter Tobin is an organised, sexual sadist, and a commuting serial killer. But how many women has he killed? Are his boasts mere bravado or an accurate tally of those women who were unfortunate enough to cross his path? Perhaps some answers can be found by analysing the behaviour of other commuting serial killers.

The Commuting Serial Killer

Robert Black was a commuting serial killer who preyed on girls, although much younger girls than were targeted by Peter Tobin. Black murdered Susan Maxwell in July 1982, Caroline Hogg a year later, and Sarah Harper in March 1986. He was finally caught when he attempted to abduct a six-year-old girl in the village of Stow in July 1990. Black escaped detection for so long primarily because of his job. He was a deliveryman for a company called Poster Dispatch and Storage, so he travelled from London to the Midlands and then up through the Borders to Glasgow and Edinburgh, distributing posters. His youngest victim was five-year-old Caroline Hogg, who was abducted in Portobello, on the outskirts of Edinburgh. Her body was eventually found in Leicestershire, dumped by Black on his journey back down south. Similarly, Susan Maxwell, Black's first victim, was abducted in the Borders, but her body was eventually discovered in Uttoxeter, some 250 miles from her home.

Black's freedom of movement played a crucial part in his ability to evade the police, because a local force investigating a killing did not tend to make connections with murders committed in other parts of the country. So local detectives could put all their effort and resources into solving their particular case, but they might remain totally unaware of a nationwide pattern that could help them identify the culprit. Furthermore, dumping a body hundreds of miles from where detectives were searching for a missing person allowed vital forensic evidence to deteriorate as wind and rain, animals and insects eroded potentially vital clues.

Ian Brady, one of the Moors Murderers, was not a commuting killer. He murdered his victims in one place. However, while in jail, he took the opportunity to interview Peter Sutcliffe – the so-called Yorkshire Ripper – who *was* a commuting serial killer. Brady tried to make sense of why Sutcliffe came to kill and to understand how he had been able to evade detection for five years. His conclusion that the latter was due to lack of 'intelligence' among the police is uncharitable, notwithstanding the fact that a number of more esteemed analysts agreed with him. It should also be remembered that the failings of the Sutcliffe investigation led to a major review of policing conducted by the future HM Chief Inspector of Constabulary, Sir Lawrence Byford.

In the same way as Robert Black's job took him all over the country, so did Sutcliffe's. He worked as a lorry driver for several companies and killed throughout Yorkshire, as well as in Manchester. The importance of his mobility – his access to a variety of lorries and cars, and his knowledge of the road network – became fully apparent in statements he gave to the police. His first murder victim was Wilma McCann, whom Sutcliffe killed in October 1975 in Leeds. After his arrest in January 1981, Sutcliffe told police:

That was the incident that started it all off . . . I was driving through Leeds late at night. I'd been to somewhere [to] have a couple of pints . . . I was in a Ford Capri, K registered – a lime-green one with a black roof with a sun grille on the back window. [After the murder,] I started the car and shot off backwards along the narrow road leading to the road. [I] swung the car around and drove away towards Leeds. I drove home as soon as possible.

Sutcliffe's final victim, killed in November 1980, was Jacqueline Hill. She was also murdered in Leeds, not far from where he had killed Wilma McCann. Between these two murders, Sutcliffe killed another eight women in four different cities – Bradford, Halifax, Huddersfield and Manchester – as well as three more in Leeds.

As is obvious from what he told the police about the murder of Wilma McCann, the link between driving and the murders was crucial. A car (and, like Tobin, Sutcliffe changed his car on a regular basis) made him mobile, provided him with the camouflage of appearing to be a 'kerb-crawler', and helped him escape as soon as he had committed the murders. Vehicles remained vital elements in his crimes throughout his killing cycle. For example, this is what Sutcliffe told police about his murder of Bradford University student Barbara Leach in September 1979: 'I had been working on my car one Saturday night and I took it out for a run. I had the urge which was in me and I went to look for a victim. It was late, so I drove straight into town and then found myself going up to the university.' And prior to the murder of Josephine Whittaker in April 1979 in Halifax, he remembered 'driving aimlessly around . . . The mood was in me and no woman was safe while I was in this state of mind.'

Sutcliffe was able to kill over a relatively wide geographical area, and many of his statements to the police included detailed accounts of the roads he travelled, descriptions of his cars, where he parked, and even the service stations he used. Of course, the fact that he drove for a living also gave him a legitimate reason to drive through various unsavoury places – such as the red-light districts of Leeds and Bradford – and provided opportunities to search for victims. For instance, he recalled, 'I had to make a delivery in Huddersfield in the afternoon. I noticed a few girls plying for trade near the market area. Two or three nights later I decided to pay them a visit.'

He murdered Helen Rytka in the town in January 1978, and attacked at least one other woman there, too.

At the time Leeds, Bradford, Huddersfield and Halifax all came under the jurisdiction of the West Yorkshire Metropolitan Police, which had been created in 1974 through the amalgamation of the Leeds and Bradford city forces and the rest of the West Yorkshire force, which had its headquarters in Wakefield. However, as the journalist and author Michael Bilton explains, this amalgamation was 'fiercely opposed' by the individual forces, which were all proud of their traditions and histories. Leeds, for example, had had its own police force since 1836, while Bradford's had been launched just twelve years later. Bilton – probably the country's leading expert on the Sutcliffe case – suggests that 'enmities and petty rivalries abounded' between the various component parts of the new force. The Bradford police, for example, thought that their counterparts in Leeds were 'flash bastards', while officers from both cities referred to their new colleagues from the county force as 'donkey wallopers'.

Did these tensions help Sutcliffe escape detection? Much of the debate about the 'botched' investigation centred on what could be called 'office management and administration'. Questions were asked about whether a computer would have helped; use of the Major Incident Room; and how records were stored and cross-referenced. Relatively little attention was paid to the issue of 'cop culture', and how this had been affected by the creation of the West Yorkshire Met. However, we can say with some certainty that the police investigation *was* a disaster. During the six years of the ongoing inquiry (1975 to 1981), Sutcliffe was interviewed nine times, and eleven times in total. He was questioned twice in the years 1977, 1978 and 1979, and three times during 1980. The two interviews in 1977 took place within the space of six days, and two of those in 1980 within eight days. But on no occasion was he arrested as a result of these interviews, or even taken to a police station for further questioning. Indeed, none of these interviews contributed to his eventual arrest.

In short, the case of the Yorkshire Ripper proves that if a police investigation into a commuting serial killer is undermined by division and rivalry – especially among colleagues – the results will be far from satisfactory.

By 2007, partly as a result of the outcry in the wake of the Ripper investigation, cooperation between police forces in Britain was much healthier. In that year 'Operation Anagram' was set up after Peter Tobin had been convicted of the murder of Angelika Kluk. Soon, this nationwide operation involved every police force in Britain delving into their cold-case files and searching through all of Tobin's former addresses in an attempt to identify every one of his victims.

Around the same time, we set out to investigate which unsolved murders might have been committed by Tobin, and specifically tried to establish whether or not he is the notorious Bible John. Tobin's age, his religious background and the fact that Angelika Kluk was murdered in Glasgow certainly led others to view him as the prime suspect. The Scottish *Daily Record*, for example, ran a story under the headline 'Cops Believe Peter Tobin Was Bible John' in December 2008. South of the border, *The Times* asked: 'Was Angelika's murderer the infamous Bible John?', citing 'striking similarities between Bible John and Peter Tobin ... Tobin was a religious man, a Roman Catholic who throughout his life has sought links with churches.'

We have attempted to find an answer in various ways, but it is important here to state that we did not set out to *prove* that Tobin is Bible John. Rather, we allowed the evidence that we uncovered to inform our conclusions but kept an open mind throughout. Our research was helped immeasurably by having unique access to both the media and the police – with perhaps our greatest assistance coming in the form of interviews with some of the detectives who worked on the original Bible John investigation. We have also utilised our extensive experience of working with and writing about serial killers to develop a psychological profile of Bible John in order to determine why he killed and killed again. We were then able to compare this profile with what we know about Tobin. We have visited the sites where Tobin is known to have murdered and where he disposed of his victims' bodies – in England and Scotland – and have walked the streets where Bible John met and murdered his three certain victims. We also interviewed Tobin's first wife – who was living with him in Glasgow in 1968–9 – as well as his third wife, with whom he fathered a child who played in the Margate garden where he had buried two teenage girls. We built up a picture of Tobin's habits at the time of the Bible John murders, and followed Tobin's trials for the murders of Angelika Kluk, Vicky Hamilton and Dinah McNicol. Finally, we immersed ourselves in the mini-industry devoted to Bible John to see what light it might throw on the mystery.

That mini-industry comprises websites, plays, films, documentaries, songs, true crime books, and even fictional accounts
of the murders, such as *Black and Blue* by Ian Rankin. Typing
the words 'Bible John' into a search engine generates a
plethora of journal and newspaper articles that have chronicled
every twist and turn of the case – from the exhumation of a
man thought to be the murderer in a Lanarkshire cemetery in
1996, to revelations about a new prime suspect in 2000, and a
probe in 2004 in which a number of men in their late fifties
and early sixties were asked to provide blood samples. Of
course, there are also numerous crime websites and chat rooms
devoted to debating Bible John.

However, when sifting through this copious and often rich
material, one point swiftly becomes clear: very little attention
is ever paid to Bible John's first victim, Pat Docker. This
seems a curious oversight, especially as the first in a series of
murders often provides the greatest amount of evidence. In a
bid to rectify this, we looked closely at Pat's murder in the
hope that the circumstances surrounding her death might provide some fresh insights into Bible John.

We wrote to Peter Tobin to ask for an interview, but he
refused our request. Nor has he ever given evidence at any of
his murder trials. However, we do not consider his silence to
be a hindrance to our task. Serial killers (and other serial
offenders) fall into two distinct groups: those who are largely
uncommunicative, like Tobin; and those who talk endlessly
but rarely provide any insights into their true motivation or
mindset. The second category – probably the majority –
develop a robust and self-serving view of why they killed
repeatedly. More often than not, the opinions and 'revelations'

they give are in fact carefully constructed to suit the nature and circumstances of their arrest, conviction and imprisonment. All too frequently, their explanations and justifications for what they did are rooted in the forlorn hope that they might eventually be considered for parole or transferred to a less harsh prison environment. Sometimes they are concocted to maintain a conception of 'self' that is more in keeping with their own sense of who they are, and what they think they are entitled to. This, of course, is why Tobin claimed he had murdered forty-eight women, but refused to give any specific details. But when these murderers' justifications for what they did are investigated in any depth, they rarely comprise anything out of the ordinary. Some serial killers – such as Robert Black – undoubtedly had appalling childhoods, filled with abandonment and abuse, but does that ever justify the horrific crimes they went on to commit? Of course it does not.

In the pages that follow, we attempt to analyse Peter Tobin. In doing so, we aim to understand what drove him to kill and kill again, and to find the truth behind his murders. We also focus on the nature of serial killing more generally, and in particular look into the circumstances that have allowed serial killers to escape detection in Great Britain. We examine how policing practices, forensic science and offender profiling have evolved over time, and how, in the end, such developments helped to catch Tobin. And we conclude that while there are and will be new serial killers at large in this country, we doubt that we will ever see the like of Peter Tobin again. Given recent advances in forensic science, it is unlikely that any future serial killer will be able to remain one step ahead of the police and continue to murder for several decades. By bringing

Tobin to justice, the British police have finally halted the killing career of one this country's most notorious serial killers.

But did that career date back to Glasgow 1968 and the crimes of Bible John? As we have said, we did not start our investigation with the intention of proving that was the case. Nevertheless, we hope that our conclusion will be as convincing to others as it is to us.

Chapter One

Glasgow at the Time of Bible John

> Any young man is a bundle of possibilities, and the
> world which is before him is like a city seen at night
> with its lights shining and its gay noise; this world is a
> beckoning, tempting thing. You can become anything.

> Archie Hind, *The Dear Green Place* (1966)

The 1960s were not kind to Glasgow. Everything that had
once seemed to be essential to the future well-being of
Scotland's largest city – the 'Dear Green Place', the 'Second
City of the British Empire' – shipbuilding, engineering, rail-
ways, manufacturing and trade were in decline, partly through
foreign competition, but also because of lack of investment
and a reluctance to move with the times. Glasgow's nineteenth-
century 'economic miracle' had been founded on a low-wage
economy – namely cheap, immigrant labour, who were housed
in quickly built and often sub-standard accommodation. Their
labour and enterprise had allowed Glasgow to become a
symbol of the free market economy that drove the Empire,
but by the 1960s all of that had changed. For example, the

Clyde-based shipyards, which had once produced almost a third of the world's merchant fleet, had become sites of restrictive practices, weak management, inefficiency and inevitable loss-making. The phrase 'Clyde-built' had once been synonymous with quality and craftsmanship. By the mid-1960s, it epitomised economic crisis and a dependence on state subsidies.

In 1947, a survey of Glasgow's permanent housing stock found that more than 100,000 dwellings – nearly a third of all the houses in the city – were at or beyond the end of their structural lives. They were damp and crumbling, with no running hot water or internal sanitation. Faced with this problem, the Glasgow Corporation (the local authority for the city) pulled down this housing, uprooted the inhabitants and re-housed them in the 'new towns' of East Kilbride and Cumbernauld. So, between 1951 and 1971, Glasgow's population fell by more than 190,000 – from 1,089,767 to 897,483. In the wake of this exodus a sense of decay and abandonment filled the city, with old buildings standing empty – their windows quick and easy targets for any small boys who had been left behind – until they could eventually be demolished. Moreover, in spite of the thousands who left the city, the decimation of the manufacturing and trading base meant unemployment and welfare dependency increased in Glasgow, as did all the social indicators that traditionally accompany economic malaise, such as infant mortality, poor health, alcoholism and crime.

As bad as all this was, though, it could have been even worse. For example, the heart of the city could have been changed beyond all recognition. The Bruce Report – the name commonly given to two urban redevelopment reports penned by Robert Bruce, working on behalf of the Glasgow Corporation and published at the end of the Second World War and a few years later – recommended the wholesale demolition of the city centre, including such iconic buildings as Glasgow Central Station, the Kelvingrove Art Gallery and Glasgow School of Art, and even more residents being relocated. Bruce's goal was to create a 'healthy and beautiful city' by tearing down Georgian and Victorian buildings and housing everyone in the modernist architecture of the 1950s. Thankfully, he was not able to realise his objective, and in 1990 Glasgow's wonderful architectural heritage contributed to it being recognised as a 'European City of Culture'.

However, 1960s Glasgow was far more the stereotypical 'mean city' than a 'City of Culture'. Above all, crime was a serious problem. One young sociologist – who would find fame through his account of time spent with a Glasgow gang – noted that, while the city housed a fifth of the total population of Scotland, it accounted for nearly half of the country's crimes of violence. James Patrick – a pseudonym used for 'reasons of personal safety', according to the preface of *A Glasgow Gang Observed* – suggested that, 'in Glasgow, acts of extreme and unpredictable violence have become invested in an aura which transcends mere brutality'. The homicide rate – including the offences of murder, manslaughter and infanticide in England and Wales, and 'culpable homicide' (to all intents and purposes the equivalent of manslaughter) in Scotland – was roughly similar throughout Great Britain in the1940s and 1950s. However, in the 1960s, Scotland started to experience a much higher homicide rate than her southern neighbours. For example, in 1965, there were 63 homicides in Scotland, which equates to

12.1 per million of the population. That year in England and
Wales, there were 325 homicides – a rate of only 6.8 per million. By the end of the decade, the Scottish rate had increased
to 15.7 per million, whereas in England and Wales it had barely
risen at all. Glasgow played an unenviable role in these statis-
tics, and even as late as the mid-1990s, while there were 1.85
homicides in Edinburgh per 100,000 of the city's population,
and 2.17 in London, in Glasgow there were 4.99. Joe Jackson –
who joined the Glasgow Police force in the 1960s – has recently
produced an autobiography of his work as a detective in the
city. Appropriately, it is called *Chasing Killers: Three Decades of
Cracking Crime in the UK's Murder Capital*.

Much of the violence that Glasgow has experienced origi-
nates from the ongoing rivalry between the city's two major
football teams – Rangers and Celtic – whose support is still
largely based on religious grounds. Rangers are Protestant and
Celtic are Catholic, and swathes of youth (and adult) culture
can be defined by their unblinking loyalty to the team they
support. 'Are you a Billy or a Dan, or a wee Tin Can?' children
would demand when greeting strangers. The trick was to try
to work out who was asking the question before replying. If
you wanted to avoid trouble, you would answer 'Dan' if your
questioner was wearing a Celtic scarf, and 'Billy' if he was
decked out in blue. Those foolish enough to try to be smart by
answering 'Tin Can' guaranteed themselves a fight either way.
While all of this might seem like relatively harmless fun, the
extent to which religion could divide a city was becoming all
too apparent in Belfast at this time. It is not too fanciful to suggest that the Troubles in Northern Ireland could have become
a ghastly blueprint for life in the West of Scotland.

In the Gang?

Glasgow had its own specific crime problems too, though. No history of the city would be complete without mention of the razor gangs, which dated back to the 1920s, but were reinvented in the mid-1960s. Such was the concern in the city about the activities of these gangs that an Anti-Teenage Gang Committee – led by the Lord Provost – was formed, and in the May 1966 local elections a self-styled 'Progressive Party' made the return of the birch the main plank of its campaign. Citizens of Easterhouse – a sprawling estate of some 45,000 people in the north-east of the city – formed a citizen action group to combat the activities of gangs such as the Drummie, the Den Toi and the Y.41 that plagued the area. Few observers seemed to note at the time that Easterhouse – despite having the same population as the much more prosperous city of Perth – had no swimming pool, library, sports facilities, dancehall or cinema, and was simply a collection of houses rather than a community. Almost every part of Glasgow had its own marauding gang, and while religion was the dominant divisive factor in the city, what mattered most to these gangs was locality. They cared about their territory – their 'turf', their 'pitch' – much more than whether any stranger they met was Catholic or Protestant.

James Patrick spent four months in this world between October 1966 and January 1967. Befriended by 'Tim', whom he had previously taught at an approved school in the city, Patrick witnessed the comings and goings of the Young Team, a gang of largely Catholic teenagers from Maryhill. First and foremost, the members of the gang cared about territory; then, in descending order, about being viewed as 'hard', drink, drugs, status, 'patter', clothes and sex. They were rarely talkative, but their clothing – or 'gallous gear' – was 'one of the few subjects where their interest and knowledge adds fluency to their speech'. They would have detailed discussions on, for example, ticket-pockets, flaps and vents in suit jackets. Gallous gear in 1966 was a dark suit with a middle vent of no less than twelve and no more than fourteen inches in the jacket; two- to three-inch flaps over the pockets; tight trousers with one-inch turn-ups; and spotted ties with matching handkerchiefs – 'for the toap poakit'. By January 1967, though, college ties were more popular. Shoes had to have 'London toes', but brogues were equally fashionable. Patrick describes the 'best-dressed man' in Maryhill as sporting a camel-hair coat, mohair suit, silk shirts and painted ties, even though he was an unemployed labourer.

As might have been inferred from the name of the gang, the members of the Young Team were in their mid- to late teens, and Patrick notes that girls were nothing more than sex objects to them. He viewed their attitude towards sex as a mixture of Puritanism and permissiveness, but noted that some girls proved their loyalty by concealing weapons for the gang in their handbags or underwear when they visited a dancehall, where the lads would all be routinely searched by the venue's bouncers. Entering the Granada Dancehall with the Young Team reminded Patrick of tough cattlemen in the Wild West being forced by the local sheriff to hang up their guns before entering the saloon – although Tim still managed to conceal a slim razor in his jacket pocket. As the evening progressed, it became clear to Patrick that while the Young Team might have been inexperienced sexually, they were much more accomplished where violence was concerned. After one of their members had been knocked to the floor and repeatedly kicked about the head, revenge was swiftly exacted on the assailants and the dancehall was completely wrecked.

A City That Was 'Dancing Crazy'

This was the height of the 'dancehall era' – music, more than anything else, was what made the sixties 'swing'. Even today, older Glaswegians will tell you that they met their wives 'at the dancing'. Glasgow boasted the Majestic, the Locarno, the Dennistoun Palais, St Andrew's Halls, the West End Ballroom and the Plaza as well as the Granada and the Barrowland Ballroom, to name but a few. The most popular was the glitzy and brash Barrowland, which had been opened in 1934 by fruit and vegetable sellers Margaret and James McIver, and was situated in the heart of the Barras, near the city centre. The area had acquired its name because it was where pedlars would sell pots and pans, bedding, old furniture, clothing and just about anything else from their barrows. Margaret McIver, who had the bright idea of putting a roof over the trading area, was known as the Queen of the Barras. Like car-boot sales nowadays, the Barras attracted thousands of local people in search of a bargain, and Margaret was quick to realise that more money could be made out of them. When she discovered that the venue she wanted for her Christmas dance had been booked by someone else, she decided to build her very own dancehall. When it opened, the Barrowland Ballroom had a resident band – Billy McGregor and the Gaybirds – and it became hugely popular with servicemen during the war. Such was its fame that it was mentioned in one of William Joyce's propaganda broadcasts on behalf of the Nazis.

Margaret McIver died in the summer of 1958 and the Barrowland was burned to the ground in September of that year. But it was rebuilt and reopened with a sprung dance floor on Christmas Eve 1960. At the time, it had a capacity of 1,900. It attracted people not only from all over Glasgow, but from satellite towns and villages and even further afield. By 1968, it cost four shillings – twenty pence – to gain entry. There were two dance areas: downstairs, a DJ played records in a small hall called 'Geordie's Byre' in a desperate attempt by the ballroom to profit from the growing interest in pop music; upstairs, a live band entertained those on the main dance floor. This arrangement was fairly typical of every dancehall in the city.

The Barrowland was widely regarded as the liveliest dance-hall in the whole of Scotland. As a result, it attracted more than its fair share of troublemakers, particularly at the weekend. Alan Spence describes a group of friends going out dancing in the late sixties in a short story called 'Brilliant'. Most of the group – Eddie, Rab, Bugsy and Shuggie – are Protestant, but they are accompanied by a Catholic mate called Pudge. They claim to be part of a gang called the Govan Team, and they support Rangers. Prior to entering the dancehall they get 'tanked up' on beer, wine and cider – under Scottish licensing laws, bars closed at 10 p.m. – and they are searched on the door for weapons. Once inside, Shuggie and Eddie look for two girls they fancy – Betty and Helen – and start to enjoy the atmosphere once 'the drink hit in and the music was loud and familiar'. Spence describes the dancehall as: 'Circular and around the perimeter were tables and seats. Above was a balcony, overlooking the floor. Eddie had to shout to make himself heard above the noise. He was saying that he wanted to go up on the balcony . . . they leaned over the balcony, looking down at the packed floor below.' They spot Helen and Betty being chatted up by two other boys. As these boys head to the toilets, Shuggie picks a fight by deliberately barging into one of them. Then he escalates the situation:

'Watch who you're shoving son!' said Shuggie, pushing the boy again.

'Wait a minute!' said the boy.

'Think yer a fuckin' hard man?!' said Shuggie, and he butted the boy in the face and brought his knee up into his groin. The boy's friend stepped forward but Eddie stuck in his boot, stopping him.

'We're the Govan Team, pal, so don't fuckin' mess!'

This fictional account perfectly captures the way in which dancehalls had become battlegrounds where young men would challenge each other and where the threat of violence was never far away. Also bubbling just under the surface was sex. It should be remembered that Shuggie and Eddie started the fight because of two girls they fancied. And in his study of the Young Team, James Patrick provides another vivid description of the sexual tension that crackled through Glaswegian dancehalls in the 1960s:

The girls looked superb in the half-light, their very young faces heavily painted and their eyes black with mascara. Some wore lime-green trouser suits, others daring backless dresses. Their skirts and 'sexy wee black froaks' were all very short . . . In the corner of the room, in the corridors, and even on the steps leading down to the gents' toilet, some fierce winchin' was in progress.

'Fierce winchin'' was particularly common every Thursday at the Barrowland, but there was an added dimension to that night, too. It was the 'Over-25s' night, which traditionally meant the dancing was better, as it was being done by adults rather than teenagers. But there was a catch. The dancers would usually be married, and prior to entering the dancehall they would have slipped off their tell-tale wedding rings and left their kids with a babysitter, so that they could enjoy a night of unattached fun. Unsurprisingly, the Barrowland Ballroom on a Thursday night was not a sedate or select place. Rather, it has been compared to a medieval joust, with newly acquainted couples gyrating wildly on the dance floor and hoping for even more on the walk home. It was a site for illicit sexual encounters where everyone knew the routine: false names and addresses would be given, and not much incidental information that might identify who had been your partner for the night. Anonymity would commonly be preserved by use of the name 'John', so it should come as no surprise that Helen Puttock and Jeannie Williams met two men who both claimed that was their name.

This was the world that the killer who would acquire the name 'Bible John' inhabited – an overwhelmingly male world that was violent, seductive and filled with possibilities. In this environment, you had to know where you were from, look the part and command respect. Violence – proving that you were 'hard' – drinking and sex were all vital in establishing status, too. And the dancehalls, just as much as the football terraces, were the places to display just how much status you possessed. Bible John's smart appearance mattered to him just as much as it did to Glasgow's young gang members in their gallous gear. And just like the gangs, Bible John had his own turf – the dancehalls. He seemed to feel that women should be grateful that he occasionally condescended to visit the Barrowland – that 'den of iniquity' – given that he thought he was much more suited to classier establishments. This was indeed a permissive society with a chauvinistic attitude to women, and it allowed Bible John's moral – or rather amoral – code to flourish.

Archie Hind offers perhaps the best description of Glasgow in the mid-sixties. It was a 'beckoning, tempting thing', filled with 'lights shining' and 'gay noise'; a place where a young man could 'become anything'. Even a serial killer.

Chapter Two

The First Murder

It was unkindly known as 'grab a granny night'.

Joe Jackson, *Chasing Killers* (2008)

In 1968 Patricia Docker was a twenty-five-year-old nursing auxiliary employed at Mearnskirk Hospital. Pat, as she was known to her family and friends, usually worked nightshifts that would start at 10 p.m. and finish at eight o'clock the following morning. Her days off were every other Tuesday, Wednesday and Thursday. Many of the books about Bible John describe her as 'an angel'. She lived with her parents – Mr and Mrs John Wilson – at 29 Langside Place, Battlefield, in the south of the city. The road, like Battlefield itself, takes its name from the Battle of Langside of 1568, and a monument commemorating events of that day still stands at the top of Langside Avenue.

A few years earlier, in 1963, Pat had married Alex Docker, and their son – also named Alex – had been born the following year. By 1968, Alex was a corporal stationed at RAF

Digby in Lincolnshire – the service's oldest base and one that had played a key operational role during the Second World War. At first the whole family lived there, but Pat and Alex's marriage was not going well and she eventually decided to take little Alex back to Glasgow and to move in with her parents. They helped to look after the toddler, which allowed Pat to get on with her life – both at work and socially. After all, she was only twenty-five. She was also pretty, of medium height and slim build, with brown, wavy hair cut into a bob and hazel eyes.

On Thursday, 22 February 1968 – when she dressed up to go out dancing – Pat was the epitome of contemporary fashion in her yellow wool mini-dress, over which she wore a grey duffle coat with a blue fur collar. The coat also served a practical purpose as that February night was bitterly cold. She carried a brown handbag – to match her shoes – and on her right hand wore a wristwatch and the wedding ring that had once belonged to her grandmother. She told her parents that she was going to the Majestic Ballroom in Hope Street in the city centre. But she ended up at the Barrowland for its 'Over-25s' night. Perhaps by this time the Barrowland's reputation was so tarnished that Pat didn't want to worry her parents by telling them where she was really going; perhaps she just changed her mind. Whatever the reason, this simple confusion over where Pat had gone dancing would have major consequences for the police investigation into her death. When she didn't return home that night, her parents merely assumed that she had stayed over at a friend's house. It wouldn't have been the first time.

Early the following morning, joiner Maurice Goodman was

en route to his garage in Carmichael Lane – a favourite spot
for illicit lovers – just a few hundred yards from Langside
Place. As he approached, he saw a naked body – which he
took to be that of a man – lying in the garage doorway. He
jumped back in horror, then rushed back to his house to call
the police. A few minutes later, Detective Sergeant Andrew
Johnstone and Detective Constable Norman MacDonald
arrived at the scene. It was the first call of their day. Their primary objectives were to determine if the death was suspicious
and to try to identify the victim. They were mindful not to
destroy any evidence and to record as much detail as possible
about the crime scene, such as the position of the victim.
MacDonald remembers:

> There had been a heavy frost that night. We arrived about
> 8.10 a.m. and stopped the car at the Overdale Street end
> of the lane. The body was lying with the head towards us.
> Initially I thought it was a man because of the thin build,
> but when I got closer I could see it was female. She was
> completely naked, and there was no sign of her clothing.
> She was lying on her back, with the head turned to the
> right.

The investigation into Pat Docker's murder was led by
Detective Superintendent Elphinstone Dalglish, who in a matter
of months (on the sudden death of his superior) would become
head of Glasgow CID. He did not arrive at Carmichael Lane
until some hours after Johnstone and MacDonald had started
their inspection of the scene. From MacDonald's observations,
it is clear that the two junior officers were determined to be

precise – 'She was lying on her back, with her head turned to the right.' They had also attempted to gather evidence – 'there was no sign of her clothing'. No doubt they would have discussed some key questions. Had the woman taken off her clothes herself for whoever had walked her home? Had they been removed by that person after her death? Had they subsequently been destroyed, hidden or even kept as trophies by the killer? They had no answers to any of these questions, and for the moment even the identity of the victim remained a mystery. Of course, the one thing they did know, contrary to Mr Goodman's initial report, was that they were dealing with the death of a woman, not a man. The initial confusion about the gender was probably simply due to shock (in Mr Goodman's case) as well as the positioning and slight build of the body. However, it reminds us that in the early stages of a murder investigation there is often a lack of clarity, and some obvious pieces of evidence can be overlooked. Conversely, other elements can be given far too much signif-icance and consequently push an investigation in the wrong direction.

As part of their initial response, DS Johnstone and DC MacDonald called a pathologist, Dr James Imrie, to the scene to determine both the mode of death – natural causes, suicide or third party – and the cause of death. In other words, what specifically had caused the victim to die? It was also Imrie's job to estimate the time of death. But as we have seen, there was 'a heavy frost that night', which made his task much more dif-ficult. In fact, by the time he arrived, rigor mortis had already set in, so Imrie was able to say only that the victim had been dead for several hours. However, he was more certain about the cause of death. He discovered ligature marks around Pat's neck, which suggested that she had been strangled. There was no sign of anything that could have been used as a ligature on or near the body, but Imrie speculated that a belt might have been the murder weapon. There were also facial and head injuries that were consistent with Pat having been punched and/or kicked, but Imrie asserted that none of these blows would have killed her.

A portable shelter was placed over Pat's body, not only to prevent it being seen by onlookers, but to preserve the crime scene and in particular any forensic evidence that might be gathered later, such as blood, hair, fingerprints, fibres, weapons, shoe prints or tyre marks. Even in the 1960s, the police were well aware that anything found on or near a body might be of great significance and should be collected before the victim was removed for a post-mortem examination.

However, while crime scenes today are invariably treated with an almost religious reverence, nothing like the same attention to detail was enforced in the sixties. Joe Jackson, who was working as a detective constable in the Glasgow force's Northern Division on the day Pat's body was found, attended the scene in response to calls for all city divisions to send two detectives to help. He comments in his autobiography, 'In those days, it was not appreciated how important it was to pre-serve the locus in as pristine a condition as possible, so all the flatfoots were allowed to go into this lane and view the body.'

Dr Imrie has never written about his work, but one path-ologist who has is Dr Geoffrey Garrett – for thirty years the senior Home Office pathologist for the North-West of England. Coincidentally, he worked on his first case in 1968, so it is reasonable to assume that the working method he describes would also have been employed by Imrie. In *Cause of Death: Memoirs of a Home Office Pathologist*, Garrett writes:

> I take the temperature of the body and check the ambient temperature of where it was found – which might be in a house, in a field, by a roadside, anywhere. This helps in trying to establish the time of death. When everyone is satisfied that the initial parts of the inquiry have been completed, plastic bags are placed on the hands and over the head of the body and tied snugly. The whole body is wrapped in a plastic sheet and then placed in a body bag before being taken to the mortuary. The body is first weighed and measured and then, before the body, the plastic sheet is examined . . . similarly the bags on the hands and the head of the body are examined. The head, with its orifices and hair, and the hands, because of their natural function, are the most likely places where other bits of important material – sometimes very small – may be found . . . further hair samples are taken from the eyebrows and pubic area, while swabs are taken from the mouth, anus, [and] genitalia.

While Imrie continued to work at the scene, Johnstone and MacDonald – now supported by other officers – tried to establish the identity of the woman who had been murdered. As might be expected, first they questioned Mr Goodman, but he did not recognise the victim. The police then started to knock on doors in the local area, but they drew an almost complete blank, except for one neighbour who thought that she had heard a woman cry out 'Leave me alone!' the previous night. Various passers-by were also interviewed, but they were similarly of little assistance. Around Friday lunchtime, Pat's still-unidentified body was taken to the police mortuary for a post-mortem. Meanwhile, a search of the area around the garage uncovered Pat's soiled sanitary towel. But there was still no sign of her clothing, handbag, shoes or other belongings.

The post-mortem was conducted by Professor Gilbert Forbes of the Department of Forensic Medicine at Glasgow University. He confirmed Imrie's hypothesis that Pat had been strangled, probably with a ligature. He also stated that there was no clear evidence of sexual assault, and that Pat had been menstruating at the time of her death. The latter fact was viewed as incidental at the time, but it would come to assume great significance as the Bible John murders continued.

It was only when John Wilson read details of the murder in that evening's newspaper that he telephoned the police to say that his daughter might be missing. Up to that point, he and his wife had presumed that Pat had simply stayed over at a girlfriend's house. Almost as soon as the police started to question Mr Wilson, they were able to identify Pat Docker as their murder victim.

Finally establishing an identity for the victim allowed the police to gather more evidence, and to draw up a list of potential perpetrators. The majority of murder cases, whether in the 1960s or our own time, are 'self-solvers'. In other words, they can be solved very quickly simply by developing a basic understanding of the victim's family and circle of friends. That is because a murder victim is usually related to, or has had a relationship with, the person who kills them. So the first people to be formally interviewed that evening were Mr and Mrs Wilson themselves. This also allowed the police to build up a picture of Pat's background, movements and interests. Crucially, the couple might have been able to tell the police of anyone who had a motive for killing Pat. And in that respect an estranged husband is always a likely suspect. Indeed, hopes initially must have been high that the case would be solved very quickly, because enquiries at RAF Digby revealed that Alex was on leave in Scotland. But he was quickly excluded from enquiries as it transpired that he had been staying at his parents' home in East Lothian at the time of Pat's murder, before travelling on to St Andrews. The police eventually tracked him down, and he returned to Glasgow to formally identify his wife, even though he had not seen her since the previous October.

With all of Pat's close family no longer suspects, the police knew that this murder case would be much more difficult to solve than most. However, John Wilson had given them one vital lead. He had told them that Pat had gone dancing in the Majestic Ballroom.

Secondary Enquiries

It is always difficult to establish precisely when the initial response of a police investigation ends and the secondary enquiries begin, as there are often overlaps between the two phases. Indeed, secondary enquiries are dependent on the work that has been done in the initial response. However, it would be fair to characterise the end of the initial response of this investigation with the identification of the victim as Pat Docker, the ruling out of her estranged husband as a suspect, and Dr Forbes's assertion that she had been strangled. The secondary enquiries began by logging all of the evidence that had already been gathered, including the information that Pat had been at the Majestic, and then developing promising lines of enquiry. For instance, painstaking local enquiries had uncovered witnesses who had seen a Morris 1000 Traveller and a white Ford Consul stopping in Langside Avenue on the night when Pat was murdered. Perhaps the killer had driven one of those cars?

The police were fairly certain that Pat had been attacked precisely where she was found. The lane was quiet and dimly lit, but the surrounding area was heavily residential. Any attempt to move the body to that location by car or on foot would have been far too risky, whatever the time of night. But the detective team still had to ascertain when Pat was last seen alive, and where she might have come into contact with her killer. As yet, they didn't even have a suspect; nor had they been able to locate her clothing. In an attempt to find the clothes they even called in the Police Underwater Unit to search the nearby River Cart – pictures of the unit's work featured prominently in several Scottish newspapers. Pat's handbag and the casing for her watch were discovered, but none of her clothes.

The police still thought their best lead was that Pat had gone to the Majestic, so the inquiry focused on that dancehall and its patrons for the next few weeks. On the day Pat's body was identified, detectives went to the Majestic in the hope that someone would at least remember seeing her the night before and could give them a description of her dancing partners. Obviously, if they were lucky enough to learn whom she left with, they would have a prime suspect. The police made an announcement over the ballroom's loudspeaker, asking for anyone who had been there the previous evening to go to the foyer, where they were shown Pat's picture.

It seemed to be a promising line of enquiry. Very early on, a man said that he had seen Pat dancing there on Thursday night. Unfortunately, he couldn't remember anything about the company she had kept. Meanwhile, all the other potential leads proved worthless: the drivers of the Morris and the Ford were soon identified and eliminated from the inquiry. So the police kept returning to the Majestic, showing people Pat's photograph in the hope of jogging more memories. But no one recognised her. Finally, the detectives decided to re-interview their original informant, and it soon became apparent that he had either been very confused or had been so desperate to help that he had simply lied. After some intensive questioning he admitted that he hadn't seen Pat at all.

Pat Docker's possible little white lie to her father and then the false testimony of a single punter at the Majestic Ballroom had sent the police down the wrong track for several weeks. By the time a new informant eventually came forward to say that Pat had in fact been at the Barrowland Ballroom, it was rather late in the day to start looking for witnesses. Nevertheless, the police paid a visit to the dancehall. But the case was 'old news', and thousands of men and women had used the venue since the night of Pat's murder, so trying to unearth any information about one woman who may or may not have been there several weeks before was like looking for a needle in a haystack. And there was another problem: few people were willing to admit that they had ever attended the Barrowland on 'grab a granny night'. Even if the police promised anonymity to the punters, there was still a nagging fear that their wives or husbands might find out where they had been . . . and what they had been up to.

Building the case required a suspect, and without any witnesses coming forward to say that they had seen Pat dancing with 'a tall, blond man' or leaving with a 'short, dark-haired man who was driving a red car', there was not much more that the police could do. Months of detective work eventually turned up no witnesses, no credible suspects, not even any circumstantial evidence. Gradually the case drifted from the news, with only Pat's family and friends still hoping for a breakthrough. In time, even their memories would fade. On the fortieth anniversary of his mother's death, Alex Docker admitted to the *Daily Record* that while the mystery of who killed his mother lived on, 'I feel distant from it. When I see a picture of Pat Docker on the television screen or in a newspaper, there is the four-year-old part of me that recognises the lady as my mother but the rational me, the adult, sees her in a more detached way.' Alex could vaguely remember walking with his mother in the park, but little else.

Could More Have Been Done?

If a profiler had been available to Glasgow CID in 1968, what might he have concluded? (This is not such a fanciful idea, because a tentative 'profile' was commissioned by Glasgow CID after the third Bible John murder – see pages 158–60.) Using the basic information that has been presented above, and keeping in mind some of the shortcomings of the investigation, what do the crime scene, the fact that Pat was punched or kicked about the face, the fact that her body was left exposed and not hidden, and the fact that most of her clothes and almost all of her possessions were never found suggest about her killer? Was he organised or disorganised? In other words, was he careful and regimented, or haphazard in his approach to attracting, killing and disposing of his victim? Or perhaps he was a combination of the two? What might his motivation have been? What could a profiler have suggested to the police that might have been a profitable line of enquiry once the investigation started to flounder?

Several points immediately spring to mind. Starting with the crime scene, given that it was very close to Pat's home, it was remarkable that no one saw or heard anything untoward, with the exception of the one neighbour who heard the cry of 'Leave me alone!' Pat's killer had time to do as he wished with her, and it seems he was not overly concerned that he would be disturbed. Does that imply some knowledge of the local area? In fact, offenders often live in close proximity to their victims. But in this case we also need to remember that Pat had only recently returned to Battlefield, and that Mr Goodman could not identify her.

Next, on to the murderer's possible motivation. Perhaps he had some prior connection with Pat – or with her estranged husband – and it is even feasible that Pat arranged to meet her killer at the Barrowland Ballroom. If this was indeed the case, then the fact that she didn't tell her parents where she was going might be crucial. Perhaps Pat knew that Mr and Mrs Wilson would have disapproved not only of her choice of venue, but of whom she was planning to meet there.

And what of Pat's clothing and possessions? They were

carefully removed, and most were never found. This might have been an attempt by the killer to suggest that the motive for the attack was robbery. But it is much more likely that it reflected an understanding of how the police would conduct their investigation, and especially about how they would attempt to identify suspects – largely through fingerprints, hair and blood samples in an age before DNA profiling. Might this indicate that Pat's killer had offended before, or perhaps that he had gained insights into policing in some other way? Such a conclusion might be pushing the analysis too far, but Pat's killer certainly knew how to control the crime scene: for instance, no fingerprints were ever found.

We should also note that there was no attempt to hide Pat's naked body, which was left lying next to Mr Goodman's garage doorway. Typically, a killer who leaves his victim's body exposed would fall into the disorganised camp, whereas organised offenders are much more likely to conceal the corpse. However, it is important to view these classifications as a continuum rather than discrete entities. By leaving Pat's body in the doorway – rather than, for instance, dumping it in the nearby River Cart along with her handbag – the killer was probably implying that he was not ashamed of what he had done. As far as he was concerned, she got what she deserved. Perhaps the murderer even imagined that his actions would be lauded. He might have reasoned that a married woman with a young child should not go out dancing at the Barrowland Ballroom on a Thursday night. Rather than demanding sex with her, he might have been disgusted by the thought that Pat wanted to have sex with him! Either way, it is clear that Pat's murder was sexually motivated. Bearing this in mind, the way in which her body was left can help us understand her killer's self-constructed life-story.

The forensic evidence that exists from the 1968 post-mortem is too ambiguous to determine whether Pat was sexually assaulted, so it is difficult to say with any certainty whether her killer was sexually competent. Pat was also menstruating, which might or might not have dissuaded her killer from engaging in sexual intercourse with her. It did provide a significant clue, though. Despite carefully removing all of Pat's clothes and her possessions from the crime scene, the killer left behind her soiled sanitary towel. It seems certain that this was not an oversight, but a carefully considered message to the police by the killer. At this point we should also consider the bruising to Pat's face, which Dr Imrie thought was consistent with her being punched and/or kicked. Clearly violence of this kind would have allowed the killer to gain control over Pat, but there was more to it than that. Aiming blows at the face is hugely significant because it defaces – literally 'spoils the appearance' – and disfigures the victim. Beating Pat in this way changed her appearance. By modifying how she looked, her killer sought to limit the significance of her body and undermine how carefully she had dressed up for an evening's dancing.

Finally, we should remember that Pat was strangled. This is a particularly intimate form of murder. Unlike shooting, stabbing or clubbing over the head, it always takes some time before the victim dies. So, in that way at least, Pat's killer was 'process focused', rather than 'act focused': he wanted to savour the moment when he had power over life and death, rather than gaining pleasure simply from the act of killing itself. When someone is strangled from the front, the killer is literally looking into their eyes, watching as their life is squeezed away. In all likelihood, this adds to their enjoyment and enhances the moments that they spend with their victim. Dr Imrie suggested that Pat might have been strangled with a belt. There is nothing to suggest that she was wearing a belt that Thursday night, so it is fair to assume that the belt belonged to her killer. Did he deliberately wear it in the expectation that he would use it later to commit a murder? Could he have been that organised? Or did the thought of using it just occur to him once the assault was under way?

It is difficult to answer these questions, but we can say with more certainty that Pat's killer was the protagonist of his own drama. Any signs of disorganisation were either deliberate or perhaps an indication that this was his first killing and so he was still in the process of establishing a routine. Overall, Pat's killer was organised. When he danced with her in the Barrowland Ballroom, he already had certain ambitions and objectives that he wanted to achieve that night – and these were deeply rooted in his personality and background. He knew that these desires could be satisfied by seeking out women at the Barrowland, dancing with them, then offering to walk them home.

So, could the police have done more to find him? Looking over the wealth of literature that is devoted to Bible John, it is striking how little of it discusses the murder of Pat Docker in any depth. Largely that is because a credible Bible John witness – Jeannie Williams – shared a taxi ride with the killer right across Glasgow before he committed his third murder. So it is hardly surprising that the police – and those who have subsequently written about the case – have tended to use Jeannie's testimony as the basis for how they tell the story of Bible John. By contrast, details about what happened to Pat Docker are few and far between. No one was able to provide a description of the man *she* had met at the Barrowland. Therefore, almost inevitably, her murder has not attracted the same attention as those that followed.

There also seems to be a certain reluctance to ask whether she knew her murderer, and whether that lay behind Pat telling her parents she was going to the Majestic, not the Barrowland. We feel that she may indeed have known her attacker, simply because, statistically, most murder victims are killed by someone they know. Did the police pursue this line of enquiry fully? It seems not. For the first few weeks of the investigation, they concentrated almost all of their efforts on the Majestic. Then, when this turned out to be a false trail, they seemed utterly fazed about what to do next. In other words, they gave one lead far too much significance, and did not explore any alternatives.

If a modern-day profiler had been around in Glasgow in the late 1960s, he would have urged the police to delve deeply into Pat's new circle of friends and acquaintances since her return from Lincolnshire. For example, they would all have been checked for previous convictions for sexually related offences. But it seems that Pat's colleagues at Mearnskirk Hospital were not even interviewed about any new boyfriends, or indeed anything else. By being so focused on the Majestic, the police had nowhere else to go when this part of the investigation failed to turn up any credible witnesses. Pat's murder was quietly shelved, with Glasgow CID hoping that it had been a one-off, and that her killer would never strike again.

The Crime Scene Today

Visiting Glasgow forty years later, we attempted to make sense of the crime scene and the neighbourhood that had once been Pat Docker's home. We walked past 29 Langside Place, where Pat and her son had lived, and then crossed into Overdale Street in the hope of finding Carmichael Lane. But this was no easy matter as the lane is no longer listed in street maps of Glasgow. Consequently, many local people are unaware of its existence. However, it is still there, albeit overgrown with weeds and littered with rubbish. Branches from the trees in the back gardens of the houses in Carmichael Place reach over the lane's unsteady walls, some of which are covered in graffiti. The lane is on a slope, and houses in Overdale Street have a view down its entire length.

Having knocked on a few doors in Carmichael Place, we learned that the lane has changed over the decades. A new wall now stands in front of the site of Mr Goodman's garage, towards the bottom of the lane, but the lock-up itself would have provided ample cover from overlooking houses. Did Pat's killer realise this? Or perhaps Pat herself suggested the spot so that they could steal a private moment?

After committing the murder, the killer probably went down the lane, across Ledard Road and south towards the River Cart, where he dumped Pat's handbag. However, the river is invisible from the lane, so it seems safe to assume that Bible John had some local knowledge of which direction to take in order to utilise such a convenient dumping site. That is significant because, after the murder, he was probably heading home: to a place where he felt safe; where he could first clean himself up and then wait for the investigation to die down. Continuing south, he would eventually have arrived at Cathcart, Giffnock, Castlemilk or indeed Mearnskirk Hospital, where Pat had worked. If he had turned east instead, he would have reached Croftfoot, Rutherglen or Cambuslang. He might even have gone north, across the Clyde to Bridgeton, Parkhead or Shettleston.

This amounts to a relatively wide geographical area, but it seems certain that Pat's killer knew it well. He most likely lived there. Or perhaps he had once been a resident and was revisiting old haunts. Maybe he still had friends and family in the area who could offer him a bed for the night. Whatever the truth, Pat Docker's killer was inextricably linked to these districts of Glasgow, as we shall see time and again in the chapters that follow.

Chapter Three

Two More Murders

Is everybody here called John?

Jeannie Williams to her sister Helen Puttock on being
introduced to Helen's dancing partner at the
Barrowland Ballroom, October 1969

If the police were indeed hoping that Pat Docker's killer
would not strike again, they would eventually be sorely disappointed. But it would be eighteen months before Bible John
killed for a second time. In August 1969, his victim was
another young woman whom he picked up at the Barrowland
Ballroom, walked home, then strangled to death. Eighteen
months between murders is a relatively long 'cooling-off
period' for a serial killer, which has led some people to question whether this victim was killed by Bible John at all.
However, such a wait is far from uncommon at the beginning
of a killing cycle. It is at the end that periods between murders
tend to shorten to a matter of months, weeks or even days.
Dennis Nilsen, for example, murdered for the first time in
January 1979 and then waited eleven months before killing his

second victim, but there was only a few weeks between his penultimate and final murders.

There are a number of psychological and practical reasons why the cooling-off period reduces as the killing cycle progresses. Practically, when a killer first commits a murder, he is unskilled and therefore more prone to making mistakes. These mistakes make him vulnerable to capture, so a serial killer who wants to avoid detection will think very carefully before committing a second crime, mulling over everything he learned the first time. Psychologically, the killer might have fantasised about killing many times, but it is only when he makes that fantasy a reality for the first time that he learns how he reacts to the death of a victim. He would not have known beforehand how much force is needed to subdue a victim, or how much care is needed to manage an attack. Perhaps the victim screamed or struggled unexpectedly? Perhaps the attack lasted much longer than the killer had imagined it would? Perhaps it was over far too quickly? Perhaps the murderer expected the attack to be enjoyable but instead found the possibility of being caught in the act terrifying? All of these elements can be incorporated into a killer's fantasy life, and so might delay his need to kill again. But eventually that fantasy world will become banal, and he will start to search for another victim.

By the end of a killing cycle, serial killers often completely lose touch with reality. They do not appreciate that their behaviour has become so bizarre that they are drawing attention to themselves, and so making their identification almost inevitable. Alternatively, they may convince themselves of their own invincibility and God-like status, which leads them to believe that they will never be caught. They also start to see killing almost as their right. By the time that Harold Shipman came to murder his last victim – Kathleen Grundy, on 24 June 1998 – he was killing every ten days. And he was caught because of a blatant attempt to forge Mrs Grundy's will, something he never would have dared to try in previous years. Meanwhile, Dennis Nilsen was apprehended because he flushed his victims' body parts down the toilet and they soon blocked the drains in the flat he rented. He apparently didn't consider that the other tenants in the house might call out Dyno-Rod.

The gap between the murders of Pat Docker and Bible John's next victim might have been due to a conscious decision to lie low until the police had put their investigation well and truly on the back-burner. Or he might simply have satiated his desire to kill for a year and a half. Either way, after that eighteen-month hiatus, he was ready to kill again ... and again.

Jemima McDonald

Bridgeton – just to the east of the city centre – represented everything Glasgow was trying to eradicate in the late 1960s. It was a place of slums, abandoned buildings and wasteland. Crime was rife, and some of the city's most notorious gang battles were fought along Bridgeton Cross and Main Street. Nearby Mackeith Street was a mix of empty, derelict buildings and barely habitable tenements. Jemima 'Mima' McDonald lived in one of the latter, number 15. She was a thirty-two-year-old mother of three children – Elizabeth (twelve), Andrew (nine) and Alan (seven) – and her sister, Margaret

O'Brien, lived directly across the tenement landing. This was a handy arrangement because it meant that Margaret could help with the childcare duties, especially now that Mima's husband was no longer part of the household. Mima was five feet seven inches tall, slim and had dark brown dyed hair. So she was similar in looks to Pat Docker.

Like Pat, Mima enjoyed dancing, and the Barrowland Ballroom was her favourite venue, partly because it was within walking distance of her home. On Saturday, 16 August 1969, as usual leaving the children in the care of her sister, Mima walked to the Barrowland in a black dress, white frilly blouse and white, high-heeled slingback shoes. According to Margaret, she also took a handbag – although this was never found – which was thought to have contained a headscarf and some hair curlers.

Margaret didn't worry when Mima failed to appear the next day – she presumed that her sister had stayed over with friends. But when there was still no sign of Mima on Monday morning, Margaret's concern grew. She remembered that some of the neighbourhood children had claimed to have seen a body in one of the derelict buildings. She thought the claims were either childish chatter or could be explained by a drunk sleeping off the excesses of Saturday night, but finally she decided to check them out, just in case. Margaret walked the twenty yards to the derelict flats at 23 Mackeith Street and found Mima's body in the bed recess of an abandoned apartment. She was partly clothed and had been strangled with her own tights. The post-mortem examination would later reveal that she had been menstruating at the time of her murder.

The police investigation was initially headed by Detective Chief Superintendent Tom Goodall, who at the time was in charge of Glasgow CID. An old-fashioned policeman who had developed his own methods for dealing with investigations, Goodall seemed to be making good headway. But just two weeks after Mima's body was discovered he died of a heart attack. Before his death, though, he and the rest of the investigating team had spotted the similarities between Patricia Docker's murder and that of Mima McDonald. Both women had been strangled after a night out at the Barrowland Ballroom.

On the Tuesday after Mima's body was found, officers again went to question dancers at the venue. Mima's picture was flashed on a screen in the ballroom and the police also promised that 'the domestic problems of witnesses would be respected' – an acknowledgement that many of those at the Barrowland were married and would demand anonymity before helping. This suggests that the police had at least learned from their mistakes when asking for witnesses eighteen months before. Indeed, they were much more successful on this occasion, and within a week they had a description of the man who had been dancing with Mima. Even more significantly, she had left with him, and had been seen walking with him after midnight along London Road – just yards from the Bridgeton Cross and Mackeith Street.

This man – whom we are certain was Bible John – was described in greatest detail by an anonymous young man and a young woman. They both said that Mima's killer was aged between twenty-five and thirty-five, slim, six feet tall, with reddish fair hair that was cut short. He was wearing a suit and a white shirt. Unfortunately, neither witness felt confident enough to turn their description into an Identikit picture, so James Binnie, who by this time had replaced Goodall as the senior investigating officer, hit upon the idea of employing a professional artist to produce a likeness. Binnie called the Glasgow School of Art, and Deputy Director Lennox Paterson offered to help.

Paterson, a lecturer in graphic design who was best known for his book illustrations, interviewed the two witnesses separately at the School of Art in the hope of extracting some information that the police might have overlooked. He recalled that the woman

> had red hair and was my idea of a typical lassie who went to the dancing on a Saturday. I let her talk about her impression of the man that she'd seen. It transpired that she had this picture of a good-looking man, in the conventional sense – tall with short hair, which was unusual in those days. To her, he was almost like a film-star and definitely a ladies' man. She could describe some of his features in the most general sense, but what I was faced with was having to compose my idea of *her* idea of his face.

Later, the young man – who did not know the female witness – confirmed many of the details that she had given, and Paterson had the impression that he was somewhat jealous of the man he described. He suspected that, deep down, the young man knew he was not as good looking as Mima's killer.

Paterson did not have a great deal to work with. Each witness was able to provide little more than the most basic physical description, so the artist was largely working with mere impressions that Mima's killer had made on two young people. Furthermore, one of them was obviously attracted to him, while the other was clearly envious of his looks. Paterson tried not to make personal assumptions about some of the features that one would have expected to see in a conventional portrait, so he left the eyes in shadow and the lips indistinct. The line drawing he produced has been described as resembling an 'out of focus photograph', but it was of sufficient quality that the police thought it could be used for identification purposes. However, there was a problem. At the time Scottish law prohibited the publication of photographs or pictures of suspects ahead of arrest or trial, so the police had to ask permission from the Crown Office in Edinburgh before they were able to publish Paterson's drawing. For the first time in history, the Crown Office gave its consent – indicating how seriously the case was being treated – and the sketch was soon on TV screens and newspapers across the country. Les Brown, a detective who worked on the case, stated, 'Few folk in the city at the time can forget the vivid portrait of a good-looking man with short well-cut hair and distinctive eyes.' Even so, we need to remember that this portrait was merely Lennox Paterson's composite 'idea' of a pair of descriptions.

Another part of the investigation involved a reconstruction of Mima's last Saturday night at the Barrowland Ballroom. A policewoman wearing similar clothes to Mima's walked the half-mile between Mackeith Street and the dancehall with a small army of police officers following closely behind. Thereafter, door-to-door enquiries intensified and the police attended the Barrowland on a nightly basis. Unsurprisingly, the numbers frequenting the venue soon dropped off dramatically. Mima's brothers and sisters even offered a reward of one hundred pounds for any information leading to the arrest of her killer – a considerable sum to an impoverished family. But they were never obliged to pay up. The investigation did not get anywhere, and Mima's killer remained at large.

In light of the considerable police activity during their initial response and their ingenuity during their secondary enquiries, why did the police once again draw a blank? Once more we must take into account the fears and concerns of those people who should have been key witnesses: the married men and women who were at the Barrowland Ballroom for some 'fierce winchin''. Perhaps understandably, many of them were reluctant to admit they had been anywhere near the place that Saturday night. Nevertheless, Paterson's drawing and the attention it received should have pushed the investigation forward. The fact that it did not suggests that Bible John probably did not live in the Bridgeton area. Despite the vagueness of the sketch, if he had lived locally he surely would have been recognised by one of Mima's neighbours, or might even have come face to face with the police during their extensive door-to-door enquiries in Bridgeton. Alternatively, he could have been protected by people who did recognise him but still provided him with a safe haven. Then again, maybe he simply fled the city.

Whatever Bible John did during the police investigation, the harsh reality was that he had certainly killed for a second time, and had once again managed to evade capture. He'd also learned from Pat Docker's murder, refining his method of killing. Mima's handbag was never found; no one saw or heard anything untoward (such as a cry of 'Leave me alone!') that Saturday night; and her body lay undisturbed for almost thirty hours, which meant forensic evidence was much more difficult to collect. The derelict building provided perfect cover for Bible John to kill Mima, and then it helped to delay the discovery of her body. But it is significant that once again the killer did not attempt to conceal his victim's body. Just as he had done with Pat, he simply abandoned Mima once she was dead. Clearly, he still felt no shame about what he was doing.

He was organised enough to recognise the advantages of the derelict building; but if one had not been available, it seems certain that Mima would still have been murdered. However, the increased privacy may well have allowed him to experiment and go further than he had with Pat. Once again, we can assume that he was 'process', rather than 'act', focused – more interested in the process of causing Mima's death than in her death itself. There is a famous precedent that leads us to this conclusion. When Jack the Ripper had the safety of a room off Dorset Street, rather than having to dodge passers-by in the streets of Whitechapel, his butchery of the unfortunate Mary Jane Kelly was much more systematic than anything he had attempted before: he disembowelled her, removed her heart and cut off her breasts and ears. More recently, the security of Fred and Rose West's Cromwell Street basement allowed them to invent and perfect all manner of tortures for their victims.

We have very few details about the state of Mima McDonald's body, but we do know that she was strangled and that she was menstruating at the time of her death, just like Pat Docker. This time there was no doubt about what was used as the ligature: Mima was strangled with her own stockings.

Strangulation and menstruation. These were becoming Bible John's signatures – messages that he was sending to the police. And it would not be another eighteen months before they received the next one.

Helen Puttock

Life is never easy for a 'forces wife', but Helen Gowans – who had married George Puttock of the Royal Electrical and Mechanical Engineers – found it particularly difficult, especially after George was posted to Bad Godesburg in Germany. Helen spoke no German and so couldn't talk to anyone she met in the street or at the shops. She had been outgoing and sociable back home in Glasgow, but soon felt isolated and lonely in Germany. As a result, George agreed that she should return with their two children to live near her mother in Earl Street, Scotstoun, just north of the Clyde to the west of the city centre. Just like Pat Docker and Mima McDonald, Helen often turned to her family when she needed a babysitter: in addition to her mother, her sister – Jeannie Williams – lived near by.

Helen – who was twenty-nine – always took great care of her appearance. On the night she was murdered, she was wearing a short black dress with short sleeves, black shoes and an imitation-fur coat. She was pretty, had brown hair – just like Pat and Mima – and was five feet eight inches tall. Helen had enjoyed herself since returning to Glasgow, regularly attending the Barrowland on Thursday nights, sometimes with her sister, on other occasions with friends. George didn't seem to mind, even when he was in Glasgow too, as he was on Thursday, 30 October 1969. On that night he was coming to the end of a period of leave, but he still agreed to stay at home and watch the children while Helen went out with Jeannie. He even gave Jeannie some money for the taxi home.

Helen and Jeannie met up with two friends – Marion Cadder and Jean O'Donnell – and all four of them had a few drinks in the Trader's Tavern in Kent Street before moving on to the Barrowland. They left the pub just before 10 p.m. – closing time – and walked the short distance to the dancehall. At first, they danced to records in the smaller hall downstairs, but then they moved up to the main dance floor where, as usual, a live band was playing. Jeannie – who had three children but was separated from her second husband – was soon picked up by a man calling himself John. Jeannie assumed he was married because he didn't offer too many details about himself: just that he was from Castlemilk and worked as a roofer. Soon she noticed that another man was watching Helen, and then he asked her to dance.

A few minutes later, Helen introduced her new dancing partner as John, and Jeannie asked the obvious question: 'Is everybody here called John?' All four of them knew what she meant by the joke: you were lucky to be given a real name by either sex on 'Over-25s' nights at the Barrowland. Few of the punters seemed to mind, though.

While Jeannie thought that her John was a good dancer, Helen's was barely able to get around the dance floor. And she formed the impression that he wasn't the 'Barrowland type' in other ways, too. He was too polite, and he didn't swear. That was so unusual in the rough, urban, masculine working-class culture of Glasgow in the 1960s that Jeannie thought he stuck out like a sore thumb. Whenever Helen came back to where they were sitting, her John would stand up and allow her to take her seat before he sat down again. That type of chivalry was almost unknown at the Barrowland, as was his 'milk and roses' complexion.

Jeannie thought he was well groomed, but that he dressed rather unusually. He kept fingering a badge on the lapel of his brown suit, and sporting a regimental or old-school tie was pretty unique for a Barrowland punter. And later, his suede boots would be the subject of some unkind remarks from a group of lads as they walked to the taxi rank. Jeannie also remembered that he smoothed down the front of his scarf before he put on his overcoat, which she thought identified him as a 'mummy's boy'.

The foursome stayed together until 11.30 p.m., when the dancehall closed. As they were leaving, Jeannie stopped to buy some cigarettes from a machine. She put her money in the slot but the coins got stuck. John immediately demanded to see the manager, which Jeannie initially interpreted as either an attempt to impress her and Helen or another example of his incongruous gallantry. The manager duly appeared, and John asked for Jeannie's money to be returned. The manager demurred, but John insisted that he should pay up. Before long, the manager lost his temper, especially when John began to say what he thought was wrong with the venue. However, John didn't raise his voice, was never out of control, and still didn't swear. Jeannie sensed that he was a man who was used to getting his own way, perhaps through studying how powerful people behaved. Finally, he asked the manager for the name of the local MP, with the implied threat that he would take the matter further. The manager told John to go downstairs and see the assistant manager, who was in charge of all the machines in the dancehall.

It was at this point that John said that places like the Barrowland Ballroom were 'dens of iniquity'. He also suggested that 'they set fire to this place to get the insurance money and did it up with the money they got'. A few minutes later, he produced something from his pocket and showed it to Helen. Whatever it was seemed to impress Helen, but when Jeannie asked to see it, John brushed her away, saying, 'You know what happens to nosey folk.'

A Taxi Ride Across Glasgow

As the foursome walked to the taxi rank, Jeannie felt that Helen's John wanted to get rid of her and Castlemilk John so that he could be alone with her sister. But before long, Castlemilk John declared that he was going to catch the late-night bus to the south of the city at George Square, so he walked off into the night. He has never been heard of since, so Jeannie's suspicions that he was married would seem to have been correct.

With Jeannie's John gone, obviously she would have to share a taxi with Helen and her John, rather than make her way home alone. Eventually, that simple fact would allow Jeannie to present one of the most detailed accounts that exists about the state of mind of a serial killer just before he kills.

Bible John remained silent throughout most of the twenty-minute journey. But when he did speak, his arrogance shone through. And if what he said was true, he let slip a few details about himself. For example, there was his mention of golf and the story about his cousin hitting a hole in one; his views on the 'adulterous' women who frequented the Barrowland; his unusual (for a Glaswegian) attitude towards Rangers and Celtic; and his comment about praying rather than drinking at Hogmanay.

Over time, two of his comments have been accorded great significance. The first explains how he came to be known as 'Bible John'. Although he said he was an agnostic and couldn't be bothered with 'religious carry on', his mention of foster children and a woman who was stoned to death eventually led police to believe he was talking about Moses, whose story appears in the second book of the Old Testament, Exodus. Moreover, his use of the terms 'dens of iniquity' and 'adulterous' seems to hint at a biblical (or more precisely Old Testament) morality.

His second significant comment came when the taxi was passing Kingsway, and he seemed to recognise a block of flats. He said that his father had worked there, and that a foster home had once stood on the site. This second mention of fostering naturally led the police to believe that Bible John might himself have been a foster child.

He also talked about the geography of Glasgow, and complained about the cost of public transport: he knew the fares of buses and of the Blue Train services north of the Clyde. He seemed to be familiar with the pubs in Yoker. Finally, he said he worked in a laboratory.

What should we make of these snippets of conversation, and the general demeanour of Bible John? When we assess this information, we should remember that all of it came from Jeannie. She had been drinking that night, and when she gave her statements to the police she had recently learned that her sister had just been murdered by a man with whom they had both shared a taxi. Both of these factors might well have affected her memory of the conversation, leading Jeannie to give undue prominence to some of Bible John's comments while forgetting others completely. We also need to bear in mind that Bible John himself might not have been telling the truth. The likelihood is that he had decided to murder Helen long before the three of them got into the taxi, so he must have known that Jeannie would soon be a vital witness in the police investigation and would tell them everything she could remember. Perhaps his initial silence indicated that he was attempting to say as little as possible during the journey, and he only started talking when he felt it would arouse the sisters' suspicions if he didn't. It is eminently feasible – maybe even likely – that the stories about golf, Moses, pubs in Yoker and so on were all deliberate red herrings, brought up because he knew Jeannie would soon be interviewed by the police.

Even so, there are consistencies between the conversation in the taxi and Bible John's behaviour earlier in the evening, which suggest that we should give credence to at least some of what he said. For example, his comment about the dancehall being a 'den of iniquity' was mirrored later by his use of the phrase 'adulterous women' and his revelation that he prayed rather than drank on New Year's Eve. Furthermore, although he had a packet of cigarettes in the cab, Jeannie never saw him smoking at any point during the night. So he had made it clear that he abstained from the two most common vices in Glasgow at the time: alcohol and tobacco.

At first sight, this desire to present himself as morally superior seems utterly bizarre, given that we know he was about to commit the amoral act of murder. However, a similar duality can be found in many serial killers. For instance, Reg Christie, who killed at least six women in the 1940s and 50s, was described as being both 'filthy and fastidious'. Later, the Ipswich serial killer Steve Wright explained to a jury that he was so disgusted by the fact that he had had sex with a prostitute – whom he was later convicted of killing – that he had to remove his condom while wearing a glove. In short, serial killers often want to appear socially and morally conservative in public – they care very much about their reputations – while in private they behave in a way that is guaranteed to destroy that reputation.

Of course, Bible John's comments about the married women who frequented the Barrowland might have been directed at either or both of his companions in the taxi themselves. Perhaps we might interpret his opinions as the main motivation behind his subsequent murder of (the married) Helen, too. Did he believe that married women who left their husbands at home to go out dancing and look for some 'fierce winchin'' deserved such treatment? We also know that Jeannie found Bible John aloof and arrogant in the taxi. Again this echoes his behaviour with the manager of the Barrowland after Jeannie had lost her money in the cigarette machine.

Menstruation and Strangulation

The murder of Helen Puttock was the third time that Bible John had killed, and by now he had enough knowledge and experience to take his time and savour the moment. He was able to express himself better and therefore more clearly reflect the inner psychological journey that he was taking, for example by what he did to Helen's body after she had died.

As with his previous two victims, Bible John made no real effort to conceal the corpse: Helen was found lying against a wall on some disused land behind Earl Street. She had been hit about the face and head far more violently than either Pat or Mima, and Les Brown described her body as 'tragically mutilated'. Her nose and mouth had been bleeding. There was a deep bite mark on her wrist and a semen stain on her stocking – both of which might eventually have evidential value, but more immediately suggested the killer's state of mind. Above all, there was a clear escalation in the level of violence when compared to the first two murders. The marks to Helen's face are particularly significant because they literally changed her appearance. Bible John tried to diminish the significance of Helen Puttock as an individual by expressing his power to desecrate her body.

Around her neck was one of her stockings, and Helen's other clothing was in disarray. There was also grass on the soles of her feet, which suggested that she had tried to escape up the adjacent grass verge before being caught. And there were some withered dock leaves between the ligature and her neck. Of course, the stocking had served a practical purpose – it was used to strangle Helen – but it also had an expressive value because it was an undergarment. Removal of underwear without a person's permission amounts to violation of the victim's sexual organs. This is often done by killers because the sexual organs help to define a person's identity, so targeting them is another way of reducing the victim to something less than human. Helen, just like Pat and Mima, had been menstruating, and it was with some care that her killer neatly tucked her sanitary towel beneath her armpit – a savage desecration.

The officer in charge of the investigation, Detective Superintendent Joe Beattie, guessed that Helen and Bible John had walked together through the back close, but Helen had grown concerned that things were going too far and had tried to run away. Bible John had then caught her and punched her about the head before dragging her across the grass until he was able to turn her over, kneel on her, remove one of her stockings, and strangle her.

Although Archie MacIntyre, the dog-walker who found the body, lived on the same street as Helen, he didn't recognise her. So it was only when George Puttock approached the police to say that his wife had not returned the previous evening that Helen's identity was established. George explained where his wife had been – and indeed where he himself had been, which eliminated him as a suspect. It was also through this interview that his sister-in-law, Jeannie Williams, came into the investigation for the first time.

Jeannie was interviewed on several occasions by Beattie over the next few days, so everything the police came to know (or thought they knew) about the events of Thursday night were shaped by her testimony. She provided so many details that Beattie was initially very confident that he would be able to catch Bible John. Later, having failed to do so, he suggested, 'I was awful unlucky . . . we never even got a sniff at him.' On the other hand, Joe Jackson – the detective who had already been involved in the Pat Docker inquiry and would now work on the Helen Puttock case for several months – offers a different view. He remembers Jeannie approaching another detective on the Friday morning and admitting that she wouldn't be much help as 'I had a bucketful last night.' Nevertheless, she clearly came under considerable pressure from the police to remember all that she could about the evening in the Barrowland and especially the taxi ride home.

The press were also demanding details, and the police – who needed public assistance – were happy to oblige. At one of the early press conferences in the wake of the murder – presided over by Detective Chief Superintendent Elphinstone Dalglish – details of Jeannie's conversations with Helen's killer were revealed. It was John Quinn – a famous Glasgow crime reporter who worked for both the *Scottish Daily Mail* and the Glasgow *Evening Times* – who coined the name 'Bible John' for the murderer as a result of the information that was divulged at this conference.

The investigation continued to focus on Jeannie – perhaps far too much, given her early admission about the state she had been in on Thursday night – and she soon started to work with the Identification Branch. Then, during one of her interviews with Joe Beattie, she saw Lennox Paterson's drawing of Mima McDonald's killer and without any prompting remarked, 'That's like him.' Paterson was quickly re-employed to turn Jeannie's description into a portrait, and over the next two or three days he produced a colour painting of Bible John. On seeing the result, Jeannie asserted that Paterson 'should get a medal' before confidently predicting, 'That'll get him, nae bother. That's him!' The portrait was circulated to every

Scottish newspaper and then made into posters which were widely distributed throughout Scotland.

In total, Jeannie attended over three hundred identification parades, and on other occasions she would be collected from work by the police to go and cast her eye over a particular suspect. She got so used to this process that she started to give the suspects ratings – a 'good' one would score 70 per cent, a 'poor' one only 40 per cent. Very few scored over 90 per cent. Once Jeannie was taken by the police to a local factory's gates to wait for a shift to end, and she almost immediately realised why she had been brought there. 'You think it's him, don't you?' she asked Joe Beattie. But then she explained that while the suspect certainly looked like Bible John, he was not the man with whom she and her sister had shared a taxi.

With the issue of identification so crucial, it is worth noting another comment made by Joe Jackson in his autobiography: 'Barrowland bouncers . . . had a discussion with the suspect while he was at a cigarette machine in the foyer. I don't know why their rather different description was summarily discounted.' Indeed, Jackson suggests that Jeannie's description of Bible John was not weighed against the statements of several other people who had also seen him at the dancehall. Instead, her image of the murderer, which was carefully constructed during Jeannie's many conversations with Beattie, was treated as the only one worth pursuing. We contacted Jackson to ask how others had described Bible John, and the picture that emerges is somewhat at odds with the generally accepted image of the murderer. For example, the bouncers remembered his hair being brown, even dark brown – not fair or reddish, as Jeannie had it – and that he was shorter than six foot. Jackson also wonders that Jeannie 'romanticised' the person who had killed her sister, which would explain why he became taller and more glamorous as the investigation progressed. He reckons that much of what has passed into history as the 'Bible John story' was controlled – and to an extent fuelled – by the needs of Joe Beattie. In short, Beattie wanted to micro-manage the investigation and was loath to accept any views, opinions or theories that were at odds with his own. Perhaps this explains why the bouncers' description of Bible John has all but disappeared from view.

Les Brown and Joe Jackson both believe that Beattie made a mistake by focusing almost entirely on Jeannie's testimony. They feel that the police would have been better served by looking for women whom Bible John had previously picked up but had not killed. In his autobiography, Brown even suggests that he might have arrested Bible John, but he says that Beattie discounted his suspect – a man who gave his name as 'John White' and provided an address in St Andrews Street, both of which proved to be false. Moreover, if a witness like Jeannie Williams were to come forward in a murder investigation today, there is no doubt that the police would accord her just as much credibility as Joe Beattie accorded Jeannie. In any event, John Edgar – the man who told Brown his name was John White – came forward following the publication of Brown's book and offered to provide a DNA sample in order to clear his name. So it seems certain that Brown didn't catch Bible John, after all.

Jackson never had a prime suspect, but he did think that Beattie held something back from the inquiry; that he kept 'something up his sleeve', as he put it when we interviewed him. In other words, part of the description of Bible John might have been known only to Beattie, which enabled him to rule suspects in or out of the investigation.

Of course, the police had other leads to work on. So, for example, Jeannie's description of Bible John's unusual teeth led to a search of dental records, and a circular letter was sent to the several hundred dentists who practised in Glasgow. A plaster representation of how his teeth might look was even produced by the University of Glasgow's Dental School. All 240 tailors in the city received a visit, and a drawing of Bible John's jacket was sent to *Men's Wear*, *Tailor and Cutter* and *Style Weekly*. Given that everyone who had seen him agreed that the killer had short hair (at a time when long hair was fashionable), the police seriously considered the possibility that he might be in the armed forces, or indeed was a policeman himself. Such a line of work might also explain how he had remained so calm when challenging the manager at the dancehall. So Beattie contacted the Army and RAF Special Investigation Bureaux and the Admiralty Constabulary. Their enquiries generated dozens of suspects who resembled Paterson's portrait and might have been on leave at the time of Helen's murder. The police also interviewed the 453 hairdressers and barbers who had shops in the city, and visited divinity schools and every church in Glasgow. Every golf club secretary in Scotland was also contacted and asked about recent holes in one. However, none of these lines of enquiry proved fruitful, so perhaps we have to conclude that Bible John did indeed concoct a series of lies during the taxi ride in order to send Jeannie, and subsequently the police, down several false trails.

More certain was that Bible John had developed a very specific modus operandi. Also, because every witness concurred that he was aged at least twenty-five, it seemed likely that he had committed previous offences, particularly sexual offences. After all, each of his three known murders had sexual overtones, and they might have been the result of Pat's, Mima's and Helen's refusal to have sex because they were menstruating. It was entirely reasonable to suggest that Bible John had met many other women at Glasgow's ballrooms and had then had full sexual intercourse with them, consensual or otherwise. Taking that theory further, it was only when he discovered that his target for the evening was menstruating that he decided to kill her. So the police checked the file of every man in the relevant age bracket who had been convicted of indecent assault or rape, but again they drew a blank.

Later, though, once the investigation into Bible John was no longer front-page news, a number of women came forward to claim that they had been assaulted after dancing at the Barrowland Ballroom. One of them – Hannah Martin – even said that she was assaulted and raped by Bible John and subsequently gave birth to his child. In April 1969, before the murder of either Mima or Helen, Hannah went to the Barrowland for a night out fuelled by alcohol. She ended up in the arms of a tall figure with whom she had sex after leaving the ballroom. But after she had accepted his offer of a lift home, his sexual advances became more aggressive. Drunk and terrified that she would be attacked, Hannah threw up inside the man's car. He bundled her out and drove off in a hurry, leaving her standing on the pavement. In *Bible John's*

Secret Daughter, David Leslie claims that Hannah's daughter, born at Glasgow Royal Maternity Hospital in January 1970, could be the one indubitable link to the identity of Bible John.

However, this seems far-fetched to us for one very good reason. Why didn't Hannah go to the police immediately after her attack, or certainly once the murder inquiries into Mima's and Helen's deaths were in full swing and all over the newspapers? It is true that many rape victims feel unable to report their attacks to the police, and Hannah may also have wanted to avoid any attention being focused on her during her pregnancy because preparations were being made to have her child adopted. However, given the enormous media coverage of the three Bible John murders in 1969 and for many years thereafter, it seems amazing that Hannah maintained her silence for so long. In fact, no one knew anything about her story until the publication of Leslie's book in 2007.

In the first year of the Puttock inquiry, more than four thousand people came forward with information that they had seen Bible John, and some five thousand suspects were interviewed and eliminated. Poor George Puttock – on home leave again from the army – became the first husband of a murder victim in Scotland to make a public appeal for help and for witnesses to come forward. Other unusual methods for the time were tried, too: an early psychological profile of the killer was drawn up; and at one stage the police even turned to a psychic for help. More routinely, over one hundred officers worked on the case and in total more than fifty thousand statements were collected. All of this effort proved fruitless. Scotland's most thorough murder investigation got nowhere. Unsurprisingly, the case continued to frustrate those detectives who had worked on it, and periodically there were reviews of what had been done – or not done – especially if new information came to light or if there were developments in investigative techniques that might prove useful.

In this latter respect, the semen stain that Helen's killer left on her stockings should have been crucial once DNA profiling became much more sophisticated. Indeed, two journalists from Glasgow's *Sunday Mail* – Alan Crow and Peter Samson – claimed that Helen's stockings had been 'guarded like the Crown Jewels since her death'. The hope was that profiling techniques might eventually provide the key to unlocking the information contained in the semen sample. And indeed, in 1996, the body of John Irvine McInnes was exhumed with the intention of comparing his DNA with that in the sample. McInnes – a former soldier whose parents had been members of a strict Christian sect – had committed suicide in April 1980 at the age of forty-one by cutting the brachial artery in his armpit.

Jeannie Williams had failed to identify McInnes in one of the many ID parades she had attended during the original investigation. However, since then, there had been persistent rumours in Stonehouse, where McInnes lived, that he was Bible John, and these had been given some credence by the nature of his death. His exhumation was supervised by Marie Cassidy of the University of Glasgow, who told the *Daily Record* that her tests on McInnes's body 'will [leave] no doubt whether this is Bible John or not'. Soon it transpired that Jeannie had got it right: there was no DNA match and nor did McInnes's teeth match the bite mark that had been left on Helen's body.

Could More Have Been Done?

Joe Beattie died several years ago, but before his death he spoke to Charles Stoddart – the former Sheriff of both North Strathclyde and Lothian and Borders – about the conduct of the police investigation. These interviews formed the basis of Stoddart's book – *Bible John: Search for a Sadist*. As we have mentioned, Beattie felt he was 'unlucky' not to capture Bible John, and went on to tell Stoddart:

> We must have missed him right at the start, and yet we knew almost everything about him . . . I was rubbing my hands together during the first week. We knew so much that to me it was just a matter of time 'til we pulled him in. I've never known a case where so much information was available, but no breaks came. We got maximum co-operation from the Press, the public and almost every other agency in the city, but we got nowhere.

Stoddart himself has no doubt that the police investigation was painstaking, rigorous, imaginative and conducted with 'vigour'. That is undeniable, and in addition to the physical descriptions the police possessed detailed knowledge about how Bible John spoke, dressed and conducted himself. There was a great deal of press coverage and an almost unprecedented degree of public support. The murders captured the popular imagination in a way that other contemporary killings did not, principally because police and public alike knew that there was a *serial* killer in their midst. All of this begs two further questions. Could the police have done more? And how, given the intense nature of the investigation, did Bible John escape justice?

It would be very unfair to be too critical of the police investigation, although clearly Beattie placed too much faith in Jeannie Williams and was reluctant to accept theories from his colleagues. Joe Jackson, for example, states that he worked on the Puttock murder for over a year and was never asked for his opinion about the case. As far as we know, nor were any other detectives. Information that did not fit with the view that Beattie had constructed – such as the description provided by the Barrowland bouncers – seems to have been simply dismissed.

Another part of the investigation that seems to have been given insufficient weight was the last sighting of what might have been Helen's killer taking the night bus from Dumbarton Road to Gray Street. This might have been an enormous clue in guiding the police to where Bible John lived, because he – like many serial killers in the aftermath of committing a crime – was probably returning to an area where he felt comfortable and in control. In short, he was probably going home. He was travelling away from Scotstoun in the west of the city, so we have three options as to where he might have been going: near to the city centre, or to the eastern or southern suburbs.

The police did check this sighting, and came to the conclusion that the man was trying to get to Govan, south of the Clyde, because the northern terminal of the Govan ferry was within a few minutes' walk of the bus stop at Gray Street. Indeed, Beattie interviewed the ferry boatmen, but they could not remember anyone resembling Jeannie's description of Bible John getting on the ferry in the early hours of Friday morning. If we take it from this that Bible John was not heading south of the river, then the likelihood is that he lived to the east of the city (far more people lived in the eastern suburbs than in the city centre). Why, then, did he not stay on the bus until it reached its terminus in George Square? Well, he would have been in a very agitated state after committing the murder, and may also have been aware that some of the other passengers were suspicious of him. In these circumstances, he might simply have got off the bus earlier than he wanted to.

However, while doubt remains about where he lived, the bus sighting clearly seems to indicate that he did *not* live in Scotstoun, or in any of the other western districts, such as Drumchapel, Yoker (in spite of what he said in the taxi about its pubs), Knightswood or the more upmarket Bearsden.

The sighting on the bus is also important because of what is now called 'geographic profiling', an area of criminology that is synonymous with Professor David Canter formerly of the University of Liverpool. Canter argues that we have to look at the significance of the locations in which an offender chooses to commit his crimes and view these places as a series of stops on a journey. The actual journeys made by the murderer are not merely movements through space and time, but also reveal something of his psychological 'inner journey' as he learns where he will find the best opportunities to commit his crimes – where he is most likely to meet suitable victims, and where he will be able to kill, escape detection and therefore savour the time spent with his victim. These inner journeys allow him to develop his fantasies and refine what he wants to do. Canter further suggests that where the offender lives acts as a focus, with some murderers committing crimes only in their immediate locality, while others travel between ten or twenty miles. Then, as we have seen, there is a third group who will travel much further, until the travelling itself becomes the essence of their offending style. Through his analysis, Canter argues that offenders who kill within a limited geographical circle – 'marauders' – always return home after committing their crimes. He calls those who travel further afield 'commuters', and says that these 'journeying offenders' are always very difficult to apprehend.

These categories are quite fluid, but they open up several lines of enquiry in the Bible John case.

Commuting to Kill

In light of Canter's theory, what should we make of the man who murdered Pat, Mima and Helen? At first sight, Bible John seems to be a classic 'marauder'. He always travelled to the Barrowland Ballroom, where he knew he would find a suitable victim, and then presumably returned to wherever he lived in Glasgow after committing the murder. This physical journey mirrored an inner one of discovery that allowed him to express who he was – his values, his interests and his desires – and he seems to have been both appalled and excited by what he learned about himself. More than anything else, he discovered that women fascinated him. Of course, this private inner journey had very public consequences of the most awful kind when the bodies of his victims were found, but by then he would be safely back at home, anchored and reassured until he chose to venture out once more. That refuge not only allowed him to escape detection, but gave him time to remember, fantasise, take stock and plan.

Where might his sanctuary have been? Our first clue lies in the fact that the three crimes all began at the Barrowland Ballroom. Carmichael Place, where Pat Docker was found, is four miles south of the dancehall. Mackeith Street, where Mima McDonald met her fate, is just three-quarters of a mile south-east of the venue. While Earl Street is six miles to the north-west. Applying Canter's research, if we draw a six-mile circle with its centre at the ballroom, we find that it includes many districts that the murderer might have called home. However, we have already discounted Bridgeton (because extensive police enquiries in the area failed to make any progress) and all districts west of the dancehall (because a man we presume to be Bible John was seen heading east from there on the night bus). That leaves Parkhead and Shettleston to the east and Dennistoun and Carntyne just to the north of the Barrowland. In the south, we have to include Cathcart, Giffnock and Castlemilk. As far as the last of the these is concerned, perhaps Jeannie's John failed to come forward because he knew the killer as one of his neighbours and was scared to go to the police, or because he was in some way implicated in the crime. That may be too fanciful. But using Canter's theory, Castlemilk and these six other districts of Glasgow are the best bets for where Bible John lived.

Why, then, did no one in any of these areas recognise Bible John from Lennox Paterson's portrait? Or if they did recognise him, why did they not come forward with information? There is perhaps a simple answer: nobody paid much attention to their neighbours. We should remember that even though Pat Docker and Helen Puttock lived in the very streets where their bodies were discovered, neither was recognised by the man who found her. They were identified only when their own families came forward.

There is another possibility, though. Perhaps Bible John had been brought up in one of these districts (or maybe several of them), but had since moved elsewhere. Perhaps he returned only when he needed to, then disappeared when he had taken what he wanted from the city. If that theory is correct, it would go some way to explaining why no one came forward with information about Bible John, despite one of the most intense and widely publicised police investigations in Scottish history. He might have lived in one of these communities for weeks or even months at a time, but if he never truly became part of it, never put down roots, never developed a circle of friends or got to know his neighbours, who could be expected to recognise him from a line drawing, no matter how accurate it may have been?

What is certain is that Bible John escaped capture. This could be put down to simple good luck on his part, bad luck on the part of the police, or a combination of the two, but the fact that he remained at large would surely have consequences. Because Bible John was not the type of killer who would stop killing unless he was caught for these murders, imprisoned for another crime, or died. He would continue to find ways to express his inner journey as a killer, because that inner journey had no final destination that would satisfy him. No matter what he did, women would continue to excite and appal him in equal measure.

However, we can be sure that he learned to change his behaviour, because he was organised and sufficiently clever to appreciate that he would be caught if he continued to 'maraud' around the Barrowland Ballroom. In all likelihood, he became a 'commuter' – in space and time, and in terms of his development as a killer. As the years went by, he would have become a more skilled and practised murderer, and his fantasy life would have become ever more extreme. He must have developed tactics to avoid both capture and drawing attention to himself, blending in rather better than he did in 1968 and 1969. To all intents and purposes, he 'disappeared', becoming just a face in the crowd – an everyman whom no one really noticed. This process started immediately after Helen Puttock's murder. Until then, he had projected himself as a cut above the rest – dressing, talking and acting in marked contrast to his peers. But that was a dangerous game to play, and he must have realised that he gave away far too much during the taxi ride with Jeannie and Helen. After that, his best option was to move right away from Glasgow, to a part of the country where he would almost certainly not be recognised, where he could find other suitable victims, and where fewer police officers were looking for him. Wherever he ended up, Bible John would be able to continue his personal, inner journey, and during the course of that journey some of the women he met would certainly lose their lives.

This scenario precisely describes how Peter Tobin behaved until the moment he was arrested for the murder of Angelika Kluk.

Chapter Four

Policing Homicide – Detectives and Profilers

Anyone who is not an anarchist agrees with having a policeman at the corner of the street, but the danger at present is that of finding the policeman half-way down the chimney or even under the bed.

G. K. Chesterton, *What I Saw in America* (1922)

Despite being a staple of the entertainment industry, very little has been written about how homicide is investigated by the police. And while the media would like to portray the investigation of murder as a rational and logical process, in reality enquiries can often be chaotic and disorganised. As a result, they might never reach a successful conclusion. In particular, decisions and actions that are taken in the first few hours of a murder investigation can have far-reaching consequences. So when DS Johnstone and DC MacDonald arrived in Carmichael Lane after the discovery of the first Bible John victim, a great deal rested on their shoulders. And that was a heavy burden, especially as true professionalisation of homicide investigation was still several decades in the future, both north and south of the border. We have already seen that Johnstone and MacDonald did quite a good job of preserving the crime scene and gathering evidence, but also that their colleagues were nothing like as careful as their modern-day counterparts would be.

That is hardly surprising, as it was only in 1999 that a *Murder Investigation Manual* was created; before then, there was no single, comprehensive guide to how the police should investigate a homicide. The *Manual* describes the correct procedure during an initial response as a five-part process: preserve life (in other words, ensure that the victim is dead); preserve the crime scene; secure what evidence is available; identify the victim(s); and, identify any suspect(s). All police officers now know that they have to follow this procedure religiously.

There have been similar advances in other areas. Computers started to provide significant assistance in the analysis of data only in the late 1980s – partly in response to the Byford Inquiry into the Yorkshire Ripper investigation – while DNA would not help convict a suspect until 1988. Back in the late 1960s, by contrast, the investigation of a murder was still an autocratic process that relied almost entirely on the skills of the senior investigating officer (SIO) and how he used his staff.

The Importance of the First Murder
It is now almost a criminological truism that the first in a series of murders usually provides the greatest number of clues. That is why we devoted a whole chapter to analysing the murder of

Pat Docker. A serial killer is at his most vulnerable when he commits his first murder, because that is when he is learning most about how to kill.

Criminologists now employ a variety of tools to try to make sense of a murder scene. In particular, 'offender profiling' has recently become a key aid to the police. With the physical evidence collected and the study of the crime itself completed, profiling – which can be psychologically, geographically or crime-scene based, depending on who is conducting the analysis – takes as its central premise that an offender's characteristics can be deduced through careful examination of the nature of the offence. In other words, by establishing how the crime was committed, why the victim was chosen and so on, we can determine something about the type of person the offender is – pinpoint his or her primary characteristics. The FBI's *Crime Classification Manual* even goes so far as to claim that 'The crime scene is presumed to reflect the murderer's behaviour and personality in much the same way as furnishings reveal the homeowner's character.'

Modern offender profiling began in the FBI's Behavioral Support Unit – now known as the Investigative Support Unit – made famous through several of Thomas Harris's books, especially *Red Dragon* and *The Silence of the Lambs*. The unit was created because the FBI invariably gathered a wealth of forensic information at a crime scene and yet had no routine means to analyse it in a way that would point them in the direction of the type of offender who had committed the offence. Before long, members of the unit were pooling their collective experience of investigating multiple murders and sexual assaults, as well as conducting extensive interviews with thirty-six convicted serial killers. As a result of all this work, they asserted that the personality of an offender – in cases of serial rape or murder – could be gleaned from consideration of the following five areas:

- The crime scenes
- The nature of the attacks
- Forensic evidence
- Medical examination of the victims
- The victims' characteristics

Then the offenders can also be characterised as either 'organised' or 'disorganised' – descriptions that occur regularly in profiles. Notwithstanding the justified criticism that has been levelled at such a simplistic categorisation, it remains useful, not least because it gives investigators an insight into other characteristics that a killer may possess.

An 'organised' offender, for example, plans his murders meticulously: he will wear gloves, bring a rope or handcuffs to incapacitate his victim, and will be in full control of the crime scene. Consequently, he will leave few clues such as finger-prints, blood or semen (he will wear a condom). Typically, there will also be few – if any – witnesses to the crime and no other evidence that might reveal his identity. Little of this is disputed, but some profilers go further and attribute specific personality traits once they have established that a killer is organised. They say he will usually be intelligent, sexually active, and is likely to have a partner. He will have a skilled or semi-skilled job, and will appear 'normal' to the rest of society by keeping his true, antisocial personality well disguised. He will probably follow reports of his crimes in the media, and will often be motivated by anger or frustration in his personal life.

On the other hand, a 'disorganised' offender does not plan his crimes. He acts suddenly and randomly, using whatever comes to hand to commit his offence. For example, he will tie up his victim using her scarf or underwear; and he will stab or bludgeon with weapons that he finds near by. There is little attempt to conceal evidence, and often the victim's body is simply abandoned, rather than hidden. Once again, though, some profilers go further than outlining how a disorganised murderer will commit his crimes. They suggest that he will live alone – or at home with his parents – and will offend within his home area. He will be both socially and sexually immature, and will often have a history of mental illness. Finally, it is suggested that he commits his crimes while frightened or confused, rather than angry.

All of this may seem compelling, but it is important to introduce a note of scepticism. First, the original FBI theory that an offender's personality traits can be gleaned from his offence characteristics was largely constructed on the basis of those interviews with thirty-six convicted serial killers. We can say with some certainty that most serial killers can't help but boast about how clever they were in committing their crimes and evading the police, but can we be equally sure that they always tell an interviewer the truth? Surely it's more logical to presume that they will say whatever they think the interviewer wants to hear in order to gain some future benefit (no matter how delusional that might be), such as parole. Second, the serial killers who were interviewed had all been caught, so how much can they really tell us about those who have not been?

Maybe the characteristics of those still at large are radically different, which is precisely why they continue to evade capture. Third, can we unquestioningly take the testimonies of American serial rapists and murderers and transfer them to different social and cultural settings?

Finally, much of what passes for profiling relies on two assumptions that have hardly been scientifically tested: that offenders will display behavioural consistency (in other words, they will commit similar offences repeatedly); and that if two offenders commit their crimes in a similar way, they will possess similar personal characteristics. Of course, neither of these assumptions leaves any room for a murderer's behaviour to change to suit the specific context in which he is committing an offence.

Developing Profiles

Before throwing the baby out with the bathwater, we should acknowledge that offender profiling often helps the police to catch an offender by pushing forward the investigation. Recently, profilers have started to see their role as not only providing a psychological assessment of the offender, but offering a psychological evaluation of items found at the crime scene, or possessions found on or at the home of a suspect, and then advising the police about appropriate interview strategies.

Indeed, we ourselves used some of this methodology to construct a tentative profile of a serial killer who was attacking young women in Ipswich in 2006. We noted that it was important to acknowledge that these women sold sexual services, and that the killer discarded the bodies of his first two victims in a stream, which would have destroyed the majority of any potential forensic evidence. This led us to believe that he was organised, and that he had planned his murders carefully. We also noted that getting to his 'deposition sites' was complicated, that the sites themselves were not overlooked and that they had convenient places to park a car. Thus we suggested that the killer probably lived locally, had a good knowledge of the road system, and was a well-known punter among the women of the red-light district of the town.

As time progressed, we developed several aspects of this original profile. Eventually, we were able to compare what we had constructed with the background and personality of Steve Wright – the man subsequently arrested and convicted of these murders. He lived in a street adjoining Ipswich's red-light area and was well known to many of the prostitutes. It later emerged that he had lied to the police about using prostitutes when he had been stopped in his car and questioned in the early stages of the investigation.

In much the same way as we constructed a profile of the Ipswich killer, for this book we attempted to profile Bible John. In order to gather as much information as possible, we travelled to Glasgow and walked the streets where he had discarded the bodies of Pat, Mima and Helen; we visited the Barrowland Ballroom; we spoke with a number of detectives who had worked on the case to enhance our knowledge of the crime scenes; and we pored over what was written in the press at the time of the murders. At that stage, we had no particular suspect in mind. Our profile – which is reproduced below – was drawn up simply to allow us to think more broadly about the type of person Bible John might be, and what motivated him to kill.

Bible John – A Profile

Bible John was a travelling serial killer – what David Canter would describe as a 'commuter'. In other words, he travelled to a place where he knew he would be able to find suitable victims. In 1968 and 1969, that place was the Barrowland Ballroom in Glasgow. We do not know precisely where he travelled from, although he undoubtedly lived somewhere in the west of Scotland, and probably in the south or east of Glasgow.

Crucially, he was not known in the Barrowland, which suggests that this had only recently become his preferred destination. The sister of his final victim in 1969 described him as 'not the Barrowland type', so if he had been a regular at the dancehall, people would have noticed him earlier, and in all likelihood would have been able to identify him. He spoke differently from the usual crowd, in that he was not constantly swearing; he dressed differently and was wearing a suit on the night he picked up his third victim (however, it should be noted that gang members also wore suits); his hair was cut short at a time when long hair was the fashion; even though he had a packet of cigarettes with him in the taxi, he didn't seem to smoke; and in a city where football dominated working-class culture, he couldn't be bothered with either Rangers or Celtic, which suggests that he wasn't a 'team player'. In all of these ways, he was not like the other men and women who went to the Barrowland Ballroom; he was not a typical punter out on the pull.

While we do not know precisely where he travelled from to get to the Barrowland Ballroom, we can presume that this was not only a journey in space and time, but an inner journey. It would allow him to express who he was – his values, interests and desires. And it would let him reveal what appalled and excited him – women. In one sense, he was travelling to discover more about himself (as most of us do at some stage), and then test what he had learned and experienced.

He took all three of his victims back to where they lived prior to killing them. Each was murdered very close to her home, where family members were awaiting her return. So they were all geographically very close to safety. This is highly significant. The desire to take his victims home – to walk them almost to their own front doors – is a gesture of protection and chivalry. In this respect, Bible John is show-ing the social conservatism that many serial killers demonstrate, and it is another indication that he does not want to be viewed as a typical Barrowland Ballroom punter. However, he is also an organised serial killer, and the final kiss after the last dance is designed to provide an opportunity for him to express (and perhaps, at that moment, resolve) his private inner journey. He made the taxi driver go to Jeannie Williams's address first before doubling back to where Helen Puttock lived. That indi-cates forethought – he worked out in advance how to be alone with Helen. These murders were not spontaneous; they were planned.

Barrowland Ballroom: Bible John's hunting ground in Glasgow. *Rex Features*

Patricia Docker, Bible John's
first victim, was murdered
in 1968. *Topfoto*

Jemima McDonald, murdered by Bible John in August 1969. *Sky News*

Helen Puttock, the third and final of Bible John's known victims. Helen's sister Jeannie was able to provide the police with valuable evidence about her sister's killer after sharing a taxi ride with him. *Sky News*

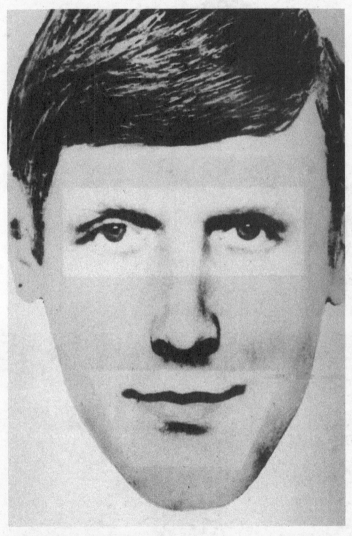

The famous police portrait of Bible John, drawn by Deputy Director of the Glasgow School of Art, Lennox Paterson. *PA Photos/Topfoto*

THE ANGELIKA KLUK MURDER

Angelika Kluk, 23, a Polish student who lived in Glasgow and was killed by Peter Tobin.
Mark St George/Rex Features

St Patrick's Roman Catholic Church, Glasgow. Angelika Kluk lived here during her time in Glasgow, and befriended handyman 'Pat McLaughlin', a.k.a. Peter Tobin. *Sky News*

Missing person posters for Angelika were posted all over the city. *Sky News*

Angelika's sister, Aneta, also living in the UK, makes a plea for information about her disappearance during a police press conference. *Sky News*

Police guard the entrance to St Patrick's church, while the search for Angelika continues. *Sky News*

The inside of St Patrick's church. Angelika's body was buried beneath the floorboards not far from the confessional. *Sky News*

The garage where Peter Tobin brutally killed Angelika. *Sky News*

VICKY HAMILTON AND DINAH McNICOL

Vicky Hamilton, the
fifteen-year-old schoolgirl
who was murdered by
Peter Tobin in 1991.
Sky News

A missing person poster for Vicky, whose disappearance
remained unsolved until 2007. *Sky News*

Dinah McNicol disappeared in 1991, aged eighteen, whilst on her way home from a music festival. *Mark St George/Rex Features*

Following Peter Tobin's arrest for the murder of Angelika Kluk, police searched his former home in Margate. *Sky News*

There was another reason to escort his victims back to where they lived: it allowed him to flaunt his power. He was emphasising that he could come and go in their communities as he pleased; do what he needed to do before disappearing into the night. He certainly possessed an intimate knowledge of the geography of these areas. He probably lived near by, or had done in the past. Perhaps his job required him to travel through these areas, which enabled him to build up a mental map of the streets, lanes and alleyways, and learn where he could commit murder without being disturbed.

Pat Docker lived south of the River Clyde in Langside Place, Battlefield. His next two victims – Mima McDonald and Helen Puttock – lived in Bridgeton and Scotstoun, to the east and west of the city centre, respectively. Bible John claimed to know about pubs in Yoker (just beyond Scotstoun) and he definitely knew about the buses and trains north of the Clyde. A man fitting Bible John's description boarded a bus at Gardner Street – having earlier been spotted walking up Dumbarton Road – and got off at the junction of Dumbarton Road and Gray Street. Did he live around there? Was he heading back into the city centre? Or to the eastern or southern suburbs? We know that the police interviewed the boatmen on the ferry to Govan, but they did not recognise anyone matching Bible John's description boarding the boat on the night in question.

Continuing the theme that he was an organised killer,

much of the clothing and other items belonging to his victims was never found, despite extensive police searches. However, he left two of their bodies in the open and made no attempt to conceal any of them (Mima McDonald's body was left in a disused flat but was also quickly discovered). All of this is significant. Bible John was not concerned about hiding his handiwork. In fact, he wanted it to be seen. He wanted to be admired and feared. He was proud of what he had done because these murders made him feel superior. His victims meant nothing to him, had no value to him, except in their death. So he wanted people to know that they were dead. The bruising to the victims' faces was also important. They were all disfigured, perhaps when he was trying to subdue them and when Pat, Mima and Helen started to realise that this last kiss was meant to be final. However, the bruising also served to dehumanise them prior to their murder. In this respect, it was expressive rather than practical violence – it reflected his deep-seated hatred of these women. We should also note that the level of violence progressively worsened as he gained confidence in what he was doing. Of course, all three victims attempted to fight back, and Bible John seems to have used many tactics to subdue them. For instance, that could account for the bite mark Helen suffered on her wrist.

Bible John left a number of clues about his identity and his motivation. We know his approximate age, what he looked like, what he wore and how he spoke. We know that he challenged the manager of the Barrowland Ballroom in a calm and focused manner. This suggests that he might have been used to dealing with people in authority and making his voice heard. Perhaps his short hair is a clue here. Perhaps he had been (or was still) in the army or the police. Perhaps he had recently been a prisoner – short hair was obligatory at the time in Scottish jails. The altercation with the manager also suggests a clear, but warped, view of right and wrong – money had been lost and compensation was therefore due. This is another aspect of his social conservatism.

The name 'Bible John' has taken on something of a life of its own, but the press gave him the nickname for a very good reason: over the course of the evening, he made a number of comments that revealed an interest in religion, if not necessarily a strongly held faith. 'Dens of iniquity' and 'adulterous' could have come straight out of the Old Testament, as could the story he told about a woman being stoned to death. Then there was his comment that he 'prayed' on New Year's Eve. Of course, on that occasion, he might have been making a joke for himself, a play on words, and really said 'preyed'. However, it should be remembered that the police believed he knelt on Helen Puttock before squeezing the life out of her – as if he were praying.

Because he was organised – and we must remember that all of these clues did not lead to his arrest, despite an extensive police investigation – there is every likelihood that he had assaulted women before the murder of Pat Docker. He would have learned how to attack women, but he did not emerge fully formed as a killer until the night when he picked up Pat at the Barrowland. He might have been in a relationship, and his girlfriend or previous partners might have been victims of his abuse. Equally, he might have attacked – though not killed – other women he'd met at Glasgow nightspots. A number of women subsequently came forward to claim that they were assaulted after dancing at the Barrowland, but none was able to lead the police to Bible John.

We don't know as much as we should about Pat Docker and her new circle of friends and acquaintances after her return from Lincolnshire. Could she have known her killer? Is that why she told her parents she was going to the Majestic rather than the Barrowland – so they would not be able to work out who she was meeting? Unfortunately, we have no answers to these questions, which is a major drawback because killers usually leave the most clues when they murder for the first time. After Pat, Bible John waited eighteen months before killing Mima, but then only a few weeks before murdering Helen. This is fairly typical behaviour for a serial killer: he starts to kill more frequently because he gains confidence in what he is doing and begins to think of himself as invincible. It is also possible that during the eighteen-month hiatus, events in his personal life stopped him killing for a second time. He might have met someone, fooled them into a relationship and then subjected them to abuse, which satiated his violent desires for a time. He might have been denied access to potential victims, for instance by being in prison. Or he might simply have left Glasgow for a year and a half.

All three of his known victims were menstruating at the time of their murder, and he left his first two victims' sanitary towels close to their bodies, then tucked Helen Puttock's under her armpit. On each occasion, this was clearly a message that Bible John wanted to send to whoever found the body, the police and ultimately the public at large. It was his 'signature' – an enduring and repetitive aspect of his behaviour that must have fulfilled some psychological need. The fact that they were menstruating offended and excited him. Just prior to attacking them, he may well have been told, 'I can't have sex with you – it's the wrong time of the month.' This could have been taken as a slight that his fragile ego could not stomach, and may even have allowed him to view himself as an innocent being led up the proverbial garden path by 'adulterous' women. He had expected – demanded – to have sex, and he was left frustrated and disappointed. It is far-fetched to suggest that he chose victims who were menstruating. How would he have known, unless they had mentioned it much earlier in the evening, which seems highly unlikely? Much more plausible is that Pat, Mima and Helen were all murdered because Bible John discovered that they were menstruating once he had seen them almost to their homes.

While we can say with certainty that he hated women, sex still appears to have motivated Bible John, and he was sexually competent, as we know from the semen stain found on Helen's clothing. This again might lead us to believe that he was in some form of relationship, which offers an explanation for why the killings temporarily stopped. He may have expressed his inner journey within his own (or his girlfriend's) home. Although, if that were the case, we should pity his partner. He would have been angry, unpredictable, demanding and dominating, and his moods would have swung widely from one moment to the next. That unpredictability might come to the fore in another way, too. While Pat, Mima and Helen were all sexually active women who were menstruating at the time of their death, we cannot assume that Bible John limited himself to such victims in the future. He was on a journey of self-discovery, and perhaps that journey eventually led him to choose victims who were not yet old enough to menstruate.

Finally, the fact that he was organised at the crime scene – leaving only those clues that he wanted to be found – suggests that he was intelligent enough to have a skilled or semi-skilled occupation.

Reading through this early profile knowing what we know now generates a mixture of emotions. For example, when we drew it up, every little detail was viewed as having equal significance, so there was no attempt to prioritise one piece of information over another. As a result, there are inconsistencies – or at least ambiguities – in our descriptions and speculations. Could he have been a prisoner or a police officer? How could someone who was so obviously different from the crowd also blend in with that crowd and become faceless? What significance was there in the way that he dressed and his haircut? How much weight should be given to the conversation with Helen and Jeannie in the taxi ride across Glasgow? Has even his nickname, 'Bible John', sent everyone down the wrong trail for the past forty years?

Notwithstanding all of these reservations, the profile reaches some tentative conclusions. Bible John travelled to find victims, and through that he embarked on a more personal and psychological journey of discovery. He was both appalled and excited by women, and was sexually competent. That meant he was capable of forming relationships with female partners, but these would not have been happy or stable relationships. He had a warped view of right and wrong, and could be chivalrous while planning the most amoral act imaginable. He was not a team player, which led him to seek out opportunities to emphasise his superiority over his peers.

All of this leads us to believe that, while he might have left Glasgow after killing Helen Puttock, he did not stop murdering. His journey of self-discovery would end only when he was caught or when he died himself. However, the similarities between his first three victims should not lead us to presume that he restricted himself to sexually active, menstruating women. Criminologists like to look for patterns and consistency

in the behaviour of serial killers, but these murderers are often
unpredictable and their tastes and desires can change sub-
stantially over time. In any event, it was probably a coincidence
that Bible John's first three victims were all menstruating at the
time of their death. In the future, he may well have started to
choose younger victims who were easier to control.

Chapter Five

The Murder of Angelika Kluk

I'd rather you shoot at tin cans in the backyard, but I
know you'll go after birds. Shoot all the blue jays you
want, if you can hit 'em, but remember it's a sin to kill
a mockingbird.

Harper Lee, *To Kill a Mockingbird* (1960)

It was September 2006. She had taken a break from reading *To
Kill a Mockingbird* – a book she had recently been given – and
come to help out her friend, the odd-job man in the garage.
After all, she was his 'little apprentice'. She felt as harmless as
a mockingbird herself: she just wanted people to like her; if
they did, she would like them back. That was probably why
things had gone so well for her. She'd travelled to a country
she'd always adored and had landed on her feet. She'd even
fallen in love. And in just a couple of days she would leave
Scotland and be back home in Poland. They took a well-
earned break in the kitchen, shared a joke and a smile across
the table, then returned to the garage. As she dipped her brush
into the paint and began working it into the wood, Angelika

Kluk cast her mind back several years – to the beginning of a quite incredible adventure.

Dreams of Another Land

Angelika was beside herself with excitement. She could contain herself no longer and insisted that her friend pull over. The car had barely come to a halt before she was out of the passenger door and running into the summer sunshine.

'I want to smell the grass,' she told her friend, giggling as she made for the sun-soaked patch of green. After yet another harsh Polish winter, the countryside had come alive again. Now it was feeding Angelika's irrepressible spirit.

Reaching the countryside had been easy. Her home was the small provincial town of Skoczow, ten miles north-east of the border with the Czech Republic. Drive just a few minutes in any direction, and you would find yourself surrounded by greenery. On their way home – a small apartment in a five-storey block of flats – Angelika could hardly wait to tell her sister Aneta about her day out.

Money was tight, even though her father Wladyslaw was getting regular work in the construction business. At fifty, he wasn't prepared to leave home and join the exodus of Polish workers travelling to Western Europe in search of better-paid jobs. But that was precisely what Angelika planned to do: find a better life in the glamorous West. She still loved Skoczow, though. The town was steeped in history, and Angelika fondly remembered the excitement and enormous fuss surrounding Pope John Paul II's visit in 1995. On the hill overlooking Skoczow stood a small chapel beside a large wooden cross. It was from there that the head of the Catholic Church had held a mass in front of thousands.

Angelika's connections to the Church were strong. St Mary of the Rosary was only a short distance from her home, and her parish priest Father Piotre Kocur had nurtured her faith. He was keen for her to know that, wherever she went in life, God would always watch over her and the Church would protect her. Thank goodness for that, Angelika thought. There was so much to discover out there; if God was on her side, she'd be guided in the right direction.

She had always been curious about life outside Poland, and while at Gdansk University she developed the confidence to explore it for herself. She knew her curiosity might lead her to some unusual places, but she felt exhilarated at the prospect of visiting them, rather than concerned. As the students began to make their way home for the summer holidays, Angelika knew that the easy thing would be to travel the three hundred miles south to Skoczow and spend her days gazing at the posters of Scotland that covered every inch of her and her sister's bedroom walls. Instead, she decided to make a much more ambitious trip, one that would allow her to touch and smell the Highlands, rather than simply dream about them.

Angelika and Aneta had devoured library books and magazine articles about Scotland, and they had studied endless pictures of the Highlands. The similarities to their home country were striking. The forests, the lochs, the history, the tradition – Angelika simply knew that she would feel at home in Scotland. But it also had something that was missing in Poland – plenty of well-paid jobs. And when Poland joined the European Union, travelling across the continent became much cheaper and easier than it had been. Knowing that she needed to earn money to support herself through university, it seemed the perfect time to make the trip. A language student with a good grasp of English, Angelika, like thousands of her fellow students, headed to the UK to work in that summer of 2004. But while most were drawn to the bright lights of London or Manchester, Angelika headed straight to Scotland.

She was a small-town girl, far away from home for the first time, and that might have been reflected in her plain clothes and lack of make-up, but she was bright and resourceful. When she arrived, she had no job organised, nor even anywhere to sleep. But within a day she had found a bed in a hostel in Edinburgh and secured a job as a cloakroom attendant and cleaner. The summer passed quickly, and Angelika earned good money.

Into the Arms of God

Angelika made her second trip to Scotland in 2005, this time basing herself in Glasgow. Well aware of all the support that religious communities had to offer, it wasn't long before she had sought out the nearest Roman Catholic Church. By then she had already managed to find a flat in Elliot Street, in the Anderston area of the city, just north of the Clyde to the west of the M8 motorway.

Anderston had changed much over the years. In the nineteenth century, it had housed thousands of workers from the engineering and shipbuilding industries on the Clyde. Tenements were built in vast numbers, with the residents' spiritual needs met by numerous newly erected churches, such as the Catholic St Patrick's. Built in 1898, the church managed to survive Anderston's 1960s facelift, although the M8 is now just a stone's throw from its front door. Its once dominating steeple is now dwarfed by surrounding high-rises. And the numerous underpasses and service roads constructed during the 'regeneration' project have merely provided Anderston with the infrastructure for a thriving red-light district. The one constant throughout all of these changes (not to mention two world wars) was St Patrick's, with its east-facing stained-glass window. It had survived the bulldozers to see Anderston's fortunes decline dramatically, but now they finally seemed to be changing for the better.

The church was just a five-minute walk from Angelika's flat. And ten minutes from there she could be shopping in the centre of the city. She had wasted no time in attending her first mass and getting to know most of the other parishioners. But there was one person she was especially eager to meet, so after one Sunday service she decided to introduce herself.

Father Gerry Nugent appeared to be a generous man. He had been the priest at St Patrick's for more than eight years and his doors were always open. Angelika quickly learned that he would give sanctuary to those who needed it most. Situated behind the church was his chapel house, which, she came to discover, accommodated a procession of needy tenants, from failed asylum-seekers to down-on-their-luck students. To Father Nugent, St Patrick's was more than just a place of worship. It could offer the most disadvantaged a helping hand to get back on their feet again.

'It's about God opening his arms to all of his children and we should try to be the same,' he would often preach.

But few knew the full details of the comings and goings at

the chapel house, not even the Glasgow Catholic Archdiocese. Some of the guests stayed for just a night or two. Others were there on a more long-term basis. Sometimes as many as twenty people could be in and out at any one time. As far as Angelika was concerned, all of this was simply evidence of the church doing its job, supporting its community. No more, no less.

Little did she know that she was about to become the latest recipient of Father Nugent's charity. Within a few weeks of meeting the priest, she was told by her landlord to vacate her flat. Soon to be homeless, Angelika turned to Father Nugent for help. She asked him whether he knew of a family who had a spare room she could rent. He did, but then said he had a much better solution. He showed her to one of the rooms in the chapel house and invited her to stay there instead.

Angelika could barely believe her luck. She had been welcomed into the local community, and now the church at its heart had offered her a safe place to stay. She could continue to work in the morning as an office cleaner, before the employees arrived, and in the afternoon as a chambermaid in a hotel, without having to spend virtually all of her earnings on rent. She would do odd jobs and clean around the church and chapel house to pay her way. It immediately felt like home and she was able to relax. Several other parishioners did not feel so comfortable about the living arrangements in the chapel house, though. Whispers and rumours about behaviour ill-suited to a priest began to spread among the congregation. But it seems that most of them stopped whenever Angelika was within earshot.

Once ordained, Father Nugent had rapidly been recognised as a rising star within the Scottish Catholic Church. His first church – St Michael's – was on a housing estate in Dumbarton, a town where sectarianism was rife. Relations between the Catholic and Protestant populations were poor, at best. But in the late 1960s, Father Nugent and a minister from the local Church of Scotland parish made huge strides in bringing the two communities together. The two men managed to instil a new tradition that continues even today. Each year, one congregation visits the other's church so they may all worship under the same roof. The next year, the compliment is returned.

Eventually, though, Father Nugent's good looks, his attraction to the opposite sex, and rumours of a relationship with a married woman undid his reputation as a forward-thinking priest with an unblemished career. In 1993 the Archdiocese of Glasgow received an anonymous letter of complaint about his behaviour. This was followed by a call from a woman complaining that Father Nugent had sexually assaulted her.

Angelika knew nothing of this. She was just happy about her new home and saw Father Nugent as someone who was there to look after and inspire her. Having found her feet, she felt it was time to explore the country she loved. But a trip around Scotland would be expensive, so how would she fund it? Once again, Father Nugent came to the rescue. He knew she was short of money, and to Angelika's surprise he reached into his own pocket to give her enough cash to make the journey possible. He also allowed her to use his credit card to buy several expensive items, such as a £1,500 laptop. She told him she needed it to gain easier access to the internet and contact with her family back in Poland.

Her friendship with the sixty-two-year-old priest went from

strength to strength over the following weeks. They grew so close that often, late in the evening, they would share a good-night hug. Soon the hugs were accompanied by a kiss on the cheek, before they went their separate ways to bed. Then, one night, they didn't go their separate ways. Of course, both of them knew it was wrong. But both were unable to control their feelings. A once shy girl had become a young woman discovering herself and her sexuality, and this was exciting, uncharted territory. Meanwhile, the chain-smoking Father Nugent knew he shouldn't be abusing his position of trust. However, despite the shame and disgust he felt towards himself, he failed to put a stop to the affair. They slept together at least three more times after that first night. Angelika never gave the slightest hint to her sister or father that she had become involved with a priest.

As time went on, she started to feel even more comfortable with Father Nugent, but the way she acted began to raise eyebrows among some of the other residents in the chapel house. Angelika and the priest would often go to the swimming baths together in the morning, and she would walk around wearing just a red robe in front of him. It all seemed highly inappropriate.

However, Angelika's summer in Glasgow was drawing to a close, and she would soon have to head home and then on to Gdansk University to begin another year. Nevertheless, when Father Nugent told her she should always view St Patrick's as her home, she asked: 'Does that mean I can come back for the summer next year?'

'Of course. You must. As long as you can put up with us,' replied the smitten Father Nugent.

2006 and Back to Being 'Angela'

This time, it was a slim, ultra-confident, fashion-conscious and flirtatious young woman who packed her bags and readied herself for her third working holiday in Scotland. By now, though, her desire to return to Glasgow wasn't driven purely by earning money for her studies or for those little luxuries she enjoyed. Unbeknown to her friends and family, she might be saying goodbye to Poland for ever, to be with the man she loved.

When she arrived, Angelika was thrilled to be back on Scottish soil. Now she could be 'Angela' again. Here it was the name by which everyone knew her. Her Polish name had proved to be a bit of a tongue twister for some, so she'd shortened it. More excitement was to come in the form of a new job – this summer she would be working as a nanny for a wealthy Russian family, so money would not be an issue.

She received a welcome hug from the priest, walked back to her old room, and within days it was as if she had never been away. Little did the twenty-three-year-old know that her already unorthodox love life was about to become even more complicated.

Martin MacAskill pulled up outside the Russian family's house and got out of the car. Broad shouldered with slightly receding hair, the forty-year-old looked good for his age, Angelika thought, and he had a maturity she liked. Although Martin ran his own chauffeuring business, he wanted to take care of the contract with the Russians personally. Because the job allowed him to come into frequent contact with Angelika. Sometimes she would pass him on his way into the house in the morning or on his way out later in the day. Sometimes they would stand for a while and chat. Soon – in what seemed like no time at all – they became lovers. The only problem was that he was married, which made his place a no-go zone. So, within a week, Angelika and Martin were having sex at the chapel house, right under the nose of Father Nugent. However, it was not the priest but Angelika's sister Aneta who first learned of the affair, and she was far from happy about it. It wasn't only that Angelika's lover was a much older married man; Aneta also felt he wasn't good enough for her sister. But her opinions fell on deaf ears: Angelika had fallen too deeply in love with the man from Inverclyde to take any notice. 'I have never missed anyone as much as I miss Martin, even though he was here just a short time ago,' she wrote one evening in her diary.

For Angelika, her diary was also the place where she tried to reconcile her moral conflicts. 'Marriage is a sacred thing but I have my feelings too. I don't want it to be a dream. I want it to be life. I want to live it with my eyes wide open. My love to you is yet so small and immature but it will grow stronger and understand more,' she wrote. 'Martin is a very nice man. It is a pity most nice men are already taken. He is not too old either, merely 40. He was looking at me and for a few seconds we felt we were the richest people in the world. I am horribly, helplessly, blindly in love with him.'

The feeling was mutual. Martin had taken to calling Angelika his *aghrai* – Gaelic for 'darling'. It had been the pet name he had given his wife, too, but now he insisted that Angelika was his true darling. He dedicated a copy of *To Kill a Mockingbird* to her with the words: 'To Angela. I will always carry your song in my heart. You are my aghrai. I will always love you. Martin.' She kept the book by her bed. The meaning behind its initially mystifying title became clear to Angelika as she read beyond the words etched by her beloved: some things needed to be nurtured and protected. She felt that their love was like a mockingbird – vulnerable and not intended to do anyone any harm.

The chapel house was a large building, but it was too small to keep such a big secret. Angelika could handle the fact Father Nugent appeared to be consumed by jealousy when he found contraceptives in her bedroom. In her diary she called him a moron and highlighted his drunken petulance. Obviously, life would become more difficult at St Patrick's, but she felt things might eventually calm down. And even if they didn't, she would be able to deal with the situation. Dealing with Martin's wife, Anne, after she discovered a number of text messages Angelika had sent to her husband's mobile phone would not be quite so straightforward, though. The cat was out the bag, and Anne was furious. Martin ignored her pleas to end his affair with the Polish student, so Anne flew to Majorca to consider the future of their twelve-year marriage. That finally generated a response, and Martin followed her.

Bloody Sunday

Most Sundays, Angelika was quite happy to potter around the chapel house, read a little, and generally waste the day. On Sunday, 24 September 2006, though, she had promised to lend a hand to the church's odd-job man. She could do with the company. Father Nugent scarcely wanted anything to do with her, and she hadn't seen Martin for ten days. The previous evening, she had sent her lover a text asking if she could see him. 'I wish I could be there, giving you chicken soup and hot tea,' she keyed in, before ending: 'love you.'

But he couldn't see her. On their return from Majorca, Anne had found another text from 'Angela' in which she had called Martin her *aghrai*. This was not the time for Martin to rush off and see his lover of the past three months, even though he still loved Angelika and wanted her in his life. So he texted back to tell her he would try to see her the next day – Sunday. Angelika therefore found herself at a loose end on Saturday evening, but only until Kieran suggested they brush up on their golf swings.

Angelika had first met Aberdeen Sheriff Kieran McLernan at social gatherings shortly after she had moved into the chapel house in 2005. He attended St Patrick's because he liked the atmosphere and felt that Father Nugent created an open, welcoming, ecumenical atmosphere. During one chat Angelika had with the sixty-five-year-old and his wife, the subject turned to golf. To Kieran's surprise, Angelika seemed quite well versed in who was winning which golf tournament. His wife suggested he grab one of his clubs from the car and teach their new friend how to swing it properly. On the lawn outside the church, he duly showed her the right grip and stance. Angelika found it fun, so Kieran decided to give her one of his clubs, which she kept at the church. He also promised to take her to the driving range and really hit some balls.

At the small party after Saturday evening's mass, Kieran asked Angelika how she was getting on with the golf. She said she had made some progress, but reminded Kieran about his promise to take her to a driving range. When she then explained that she would be travelling back to Poland in a few days' time, he agreed that they should go that night. Excited, Angelika ran to get her golf club, but first she went to the garage to see Pat, the church handyman. She had been helping him to build a shed earlier that evening. Pat said he could manage fine without her, and told her to have fun.

Angelika and Kieran only had a short practice session because the Bishopbriggs range closed at 10 p.m. So they were soon back at the church, and they bumped into Pat in the garage. Angelika boasted, 'Mr McLernan tells me I have a good backswing.'

Keen for Kieran to have her email address so they could keep in touch once she went back to Poland, Angelika raced into the chapel house to find a pen and paper, leaving the two men chatting amicably. Returning with her email address on a slip of paper, she asked for Kieran's in return and he obliged. Then, once she had walked him to his car, she hugged him goodbye. In return, he reached into the car and pulled out a packet of 'dreamcatchers' – a traditional gift for children he'd brought back from a recent trip to Canada. He gave one to Angelika, telling her the net would trap all her bad dreams, while all the good ones would filter through. Little did either of them know that her nightmare was soon to begin.

On Sunday afternoon, Angelika set out to find Pat, feeling a touch guilty about leaving him to work alone on the shed the previous night.

Pat McLaughlin had turned up on the doorstep of St Patrick's roughly two months earlier. In keeping with Father

Nugent's generous open-door policy, the homeless sixty-year-old was given shelter and food. One of the many support groups the priest ran was called the Loaves and Fishes Group, which provided food and fellowship for the homeless. Like Angelika, Pat had a solid work ethic – he told Father Nugent that he was grateful to the church, but he would pay his way if he was going to stay. He immediately offered to paint a room in the chapel house, and soon it became apparent that he was a skilled handyman who knew about carpentry and electrical wiring as well as painting and decorating. Before long he was doing odd jobs all around the church, whenever they were needed. And he was always well turned out, which sometimes led Angelika to wonder if he had ever really been homeless at all.

Pat had the physical ability of someone much younger than sixty, and he was lean and fit. But his age was given away by his greying hair and a face that had seen a lot of life. But the rest of the residents at St Patrick's were only able to guess at the story that lay behind the wrinkles around his dark, piercing eyes and on the rest of his face, because Pat never shared any of his past with them. Father Nugent didn't like to press him. He felt he would find out in good time.

'Ah, my little apprentice, how are we today?' said Pat, dressed in his blue overalls, pausing for a moment when Angelika walked into the garage. He had made considerable progress painting the shed, but she would lend a hand where she could. Before long, though, Pat said it was time for a tea break, and they both moved into the church kitchen and sat down at the table.

Midday mass had just come to an end and some of the congregation had gathered for refreshments and to hear the priest tell them news of a recent donation. While Pat and Angelika chatted over their steaming cups of tea, lollipop lady and faithful church volunteer Marie Devine entered the kitchen and paused briefly before leaving to go home. It was already three o'clock, she would have to be back by six, and there were things to do. Bidding farewell, she left the pair to their conversation.

But they had work to do too, and Pat seemed unusually eager to return to the garage. They had scarcely got back inside before he clubbed Angelika on the back of the head. The force sent her flying forwards on to the floor. The acute pain caused her to raise her hand instinctively to protect herself, but a second blow followed, breaking one of her fingers and causing her to pull her hand away again. Then there was another blow. And another. In all, Pat McLaughlin hit Angelika Kluk six times on the back and side of her head. He did so with such force that he penetrated Angelika's scalp, exposing the fractured skull beneath.

As McLaughlin lifted the blood-soaked table leg for the final time, some of the deep red liquid sprayed over the pillar next to him and even on to the ceiling. The blow rendered Angelika unconscious on the garage floor. By now, she was also bleeding profusely from her wounds. McLaughlin now took the opportunity to render his 'little apprentice' incapable of defending herself if she came around. He bound her wrists and stuffed a piece of cloth into her mouth to act as a gag. Then he wrapped yellow insulation tape around her head. Her passivity also gave him the opportunity to put into practice the sexual fantasies he had long held about Angelika. He had dreamed of having sex with her ever since he'd arrived at St Patrick's.

But Angelika was not unconscious for long. Despite her injuries and her bindings, she began to fight back. That was when her assailant grabbed a knife. Looking into Angelika's eyes, he began to stab her in the chest, and sliced through her shielding hands as she desperately tried to defend herself. He stabbed her nineteen times in total – sixteen times in the chest. Ten of the chest wounds were made in very quick succession.

By now, McLaughlin was dripping with sweat as he leaned over his victim. But there was more to be done: he needed somewhere to hide the body, and he had to get rid of any evidence. He had a place in mind for the first of these tasks, but how could he get Angelika there without leaving a trail of blood? He grabbed the plastic sheeting and black bin-liner he'd been using to prevent paint splashing on the floor. Spreading them out next to Angelika, he knelt down to lever her into position on top of the sheeting, but as he did so the pool of blood began to soak into his trousers. Nevertheless, with Angelika in the plastic, he began dragging.

He had identified the perfect hiding-place some time before. His job as the church's handyman meant that he knew the building better than most. If there was ever any discussion about electrics or plumbing, he would be consulted. Recently, some of the volunteers had asked Father Nugent to look into installing a water pipe between the kitchen and a room at the back of the church where they held meetings. They were growing tired of having to use buckets to fill up their urn. To access the maze of water pipes running underneath the floor of the church, there was a hatch just outside the confessional box. It was usually covered with a rug, so only the cleaners –

and Pat McLaughlin – knew it was there. McLaughlin reckoned Angelika's body could lay undiscovered down there for weeks, if not longer.

Having dragged the dead weight through the church to the confessional box, he pulled back the carpet, inserted his finger into the brass ring-catch and lifted the hatch. Then it was a fairly easy job to funnel his eight-stone victim – still bound and gagged – into the three-foot-deep pit. Before closing the hatch, he also threw the plastic sheeting on top of her. Calmly, he then returned to the garage, where he knew few people would disturb him, and began to eradicate every trace of the murder that had just taken place. Next he would take a shower and get rid of the trousers that were soaked with Angelika's blood. When he was finally satisfied with the clean-up work in the garage, he headed into the chapel house. He had Angelika's mobile phone in his pocket.

Mockingbird Sings No More

Martin Macaskill dialled Angelika's mobile number for the eighteenth time. Yet again it was either not answered or went straight to voicemail. He had already left several messages saying how worried he was and pleading with her to get in touch, and he finally decided that this was more than Angelika just giving him the cold shoulder because he had refused to see her the night before. Consequently, he went to St Patrick's that evening, but his *aghrai* was nowhere to be seen.

By Monday morning, the shed that McLaughlin and Angelika had been working on had been placed in the church yard. When Marie Devine arrived at the church, she noticed that it still lacked a door and a window. She asked McLaughlin when the work would be done, but he said he could not get started on it as 'my apprentice hasn't turned up yet'.

One person who did turn up that Monday was Angelika's boyfriend. Martin had called his lover's mobile phone another twenty times but had still received no reply. Angelika was due to head back to Poland the following weekend, and in spite of all that had happened over the last couple of weeks, he knew she wouldn't leave without saying goodbye. He texted her again to say he was 'really, really scared' and 'almost suicidal with worry'. Still no response, so he returned to the church. By then, he'd called Aneta, who was also living in Glasgow that summer, and together they searched her younger sister's bedroom. Most of Angelika's personal effects were still there and seemingly untouched – her laptop, handbag, bank cards and, crucially, her passport and return plane ticket to Gdansk. All that was missing was her mobile phone. Aneta even established that all of her sister's coats and jumpers were there, so it seemed unlikely that she had simply left the church to have some time to herself.

Sitting at a table in the chapel house with a friend whom he had asked for help in putting the finishing touches to the shed, McLaughlin could hear Martin and Aneta growing increasingly frantic. The odd-job man's friend asked what all the commotion was about. Calmly, and without a hint of guilt, McLaughlin told him that the man's girlfriend was missing.

Martin and Aneta were fearing the worst. Initially, they discussed contacting all of Glasgow's hospitals in case Angelika had been in an accident, but instead Martin decided to call the police.

An hour later, two constables arrived at the church to be

met by Martin MacAskill, Father Nugent and Aneta Kluk. Despite a thorough search of the premises, Angelika was nowhere to be seen. Everyone who was at the church, including Pat McLaughlin, gave statements to the police. No one seemed to know where Angelika might be. Not even the calmest of all the interviewees – McLaughlin – who knew that the answer lay barely fifty yards away.

By the time the police left, it was late, and the day had been emotionally draining, so everyone agreed they would try to get some sleep, get up early and start looking again the next day. Martin and Aneta left the church, each hoping that Angelika might appear from nowhere and reveal that all of this had just been a silly misunderstanding. Deep down, though, both felt something disastrous had happened.

Early on the Tuesday morning, perhaps thinking that St Patrick's would soon be crawling with police and reporters, Pat McLaughlin quietly gathered together his few belongings and left before anyone was up and around. He had decided to lie low in the centre of Glasgow until dark. In the evening, his mobile phone rang, displaying a friend's number whom he had agreed to meet that day in the city. But McLaughlin had never had any intention of showing up. The night was well and truly set in as he arrived at St Andrew Square bus station in Edinburgh. He would not be seeing his friend, or returning to St Patrick's, any time soon.

Back at the church, Father Nugent had soon realised that the handyman had failed to turn up to work, and his calls to the man's mobile to chase him up had gone unanswered all morning. McLaughlin had often complained of a heart condition to the priest, so Father Nugent had begun to fear for the man's safety. Perhaps the stress of Angelika's disappearance had aggravated it?

News that the twenty-three-year-old was missing had spread quickly, and soon reporters did indeed begin to arrive at St Patrick's and start asking questions. The police had made it clear that they were desperate for Pat McLaughlin to come forward – they had been unable to trace him since speaking to him on Monday evening. Soon they issued a photograph of the handyman. Their enquiries had revealed that he was probably the last person to see Angelika – who at that stage was still classified as 'missing'.

Openly weeping in front of the gathered journalists, Martin MacAskill made repeated requests for anyone with information about 'Angela's' whereabouts to come forward. Even Anne joined in the hunt for her husband's missing lover – handing out fliers appealing for information in the local area. 'Angela, whatever it is, just come back. If you can, come back. You know I love you. More than anything else, I just want you to be safe and well,' pleaded Martin from the pages of the *Glasgow Herald*. In an interview with BBC Scotland, he said: 'Her enthusiasm for life and absolute passion for everything, passion for learning, enthusiasm for everything she came across was infectious, it was wonderful to see. She was just one of the people who shone.'

Father Nugent joined in the tributes to Angelika: 'She got involved in this community in an amazing way. She was full of life, a serious student, loved Scotland, wanted to learn, wanted to grow; life was a great challenge for her,' he said. 'She took part in everything and she said to me once, "You know, Father, this is like home for me." I would think that people admired her because she was taking life on and meeting it with great gusto and charm.'

Significantly, Father Nugent talked of Angelika in the past tense. By the time he gave the interview, hope was fading for the Polish student. He concluded by saying: 'As each day goes on, we're praying very much for her.'

29 September 2006

Police continued to search the church, chapel house and surrounding land for clues about the Polish girl's disappearance. Before long, they found a table leg stained with Angelika's blood and several blood-soaked towels in the church grounds. Then, in a bin, they found a pair of discarded jeans. The left knee was also covered in Angelika's blood. But for several days there was still no sign of her body.

Then, on the Friday, a forensics officer pulled at the brass ring and began to lift the hatch next to the confessional box. As the hatch opened wide, several officers recoiled as the horror of what lay below was exposed. Angelika's hands were still bound, and she was lying on her back with her legs bent underneath her. The insulating tape holding the gag in place had been wrapped so tightly that her face had become distorted. Wrapped inside the bin-liner that was lying on top of her, officers found a bloodstained kitchen knife.

With all the evidence bagged up and the body removed by a coroner's ambulance, the police started to assess how careful Angelika's killer had been. It wasn't long before they had their answer. They soon learned that Angelika had had sex shortly before her death – the large amount of semen that was available for analysis pointed to that. But even if the DNA profile generated by the semen matched that of the odd-job man who had vanished so suspiciously from the church, it would not prove that he'd killed her.

However, fingerprints would be far more conclusive. Using a chemical powder, forensic scientists were able to locate finger- and palm-prints on the plastic sheeting and bin-liner. If all of those prints turned out to belong to the same person, the police would almost certainly have their killer. Finger-prints were also found on the insulation tape that had been wrapped around Angelika's head, and the forensics team man-aged to obtain a mixed DNA profile from the cloth that had been forced into her mouth. Skin recovered from inside the blood-covered jeans found discarded in the church grounds would provide another DNA profile. Everything was pointing towards Pat McLaughlin being the perpetrator of the frenzied sex-attack.

But as the investigation kicked into top gear, the police made their most shocking discovery yet. While they continued to search for the handyman from the church, they came to realise that his name was not Pat McLaughlin. It was Peter Tobin – a registered sex offender whom they had wanted to question for over a year.

Having been released from an English prison in 2004 after serving ten years for a horrific attack on two fourteen-year-old girls, Tobin had moved back to Paisley in his native Scotland. But within ten months the police had lost track of him. They had issued a warrant for his arrest after he failed to notify them of a change of address. Neighbours had also blown the whis-tle on a man they were convinced was carrying on with an under-age girl. But by the time the police had raided Tobin's

Paisley home, he was long gone. He had eventually found refuge within a religious community that was happy not to ask too many questions. A new identity had allowed him to exploit the welcoming nature of St Patrick's to the full.

Another Day, Another Identity

Although he was in London, far away from his native Scotland, in another sense Peter Tobin was in familiar territory. Whenever he had done 'bad' things before, he had always tried to put as much distance between himself and his misdemeanours. And this time was no different. But with little money and nowhere to sleep, he would have to employ his best acting skills – the kind he'd used for the past few months to fool the people at St Patrick's. Just as a child feigns injury to limit the punishment they know is about to be meted out, Tobin liked to play the wounded soldier. On this occasion he walked into the National Neurology and Neurosurgery Hospital complaining of chest pains and weakness down his left side. He knew that the police would be looking for him (or at least Pat McLaughlin) by now, so he adopted yet another false identity: James Kelly. But a heart attack was not quite so easy to fake, as Tobin would quickly discover. Dr Nick Losseff, the consultant neurologist, could find nothing in his patient's test results to explain the chest pains. Moreover, Mr Kelly seemed very reluctant to make eye contact when the two men discussed them, and the doctor soon suspected that both the symptoms and the name were fictitious.

Shortly after Dr Losseff had left the room, a male nurse came to check on the patient. 'Good morning, Mr Kelly, my name is Alan. How are you feeling today? Any better?' He then barely uttered another word. He just seemed to stare straight into the patient's face while doing a few routine tasks around the bed. After a minute or so, he left. But soon he was back. This time, though, he was wearing his police jacket.

'I knew you were the police,' said Tobin. 'I am relieved you are here.'

'Are you—?'

But before PC Alan Murray of the Metropolitan Police could complete his question, the reply was fired back at him: 'Peter Tobin? Yes. You have been looking for me.' Then, as PC Murray cautioned and arrested Tobin, the convicted sex offender continued: 'Kent Police and Met Police are looking for me for murder. I'm surrendering myself to you, PC 227EK, by name of Alan.'

Pictures of Tobin's face had been published widely in newspapers and even broadcast on television, so it was hardly surprising that a real nurse had recognised the patient with the inexplicable chest pains and had called the police. PC Murray, with the help of a police photo, had merely confirmed that James Kelly was indeed the church handyman. Tobin's watch was later tested by forensic scientists, who found tiny specs of Angelika's blood on the face and buckle.

Angelika had thought she had fallen into the arms of God when she arrived at St Patrick's. In fact, she had fallen into the clutches of an evil killer who bound her, gagged her, raped her and discarded her lifeless body beneath the very place she felt was her armour against the unknown. But Peter Tobin would never be able to indulge his violent sexual urges again. A year later in an Edinburgh court, Judge Lord Menzies described

Tobin as 'an evil man' and sentenced him to a minimum of twenty-one years in prison.

But the police's interest in Tobin did not end there. His conviction served as a springboard. The Angelika Kluk investigation had revealed that Tobin had used thirty-eight different mobile phone SIM cards and had travelled the length and breadth of the country. The police started to fear that he could have killed many times before, and forces throughout the UK were encouraged to re-examine any cold cases in which he might have been involved. For Essex Police, that meant taking a fresh look at the disappearance of eighteen-year-old Dinah McNicol in 1991. That fresh look revealed a familiar name: of the two thousand potential suspects from the original investigation, one was Peter Tobin. Meanwhile, Strathclyde Police discovered that Tobin had been living in Bathgate when fifteen-year-old Vicky Hamilton disappeared, also in 1991. Further police enquiries would ultimately grant at least a modicum of closure to two families who had been wondering what had happened to Dinah and Vicky for sixteen years.

It is safe to say that if Angelika Kluk had never made her trip to Scotland, the true extent of Peter Tobin's evil might never have been discovered.

Peter Tobin/Bible John?

The police eventually proved that Peter Tobin had murdered women as far back as the early 1990s. Meanwhile, profilers developed a detailed understanding of when and how he killed. But could he be the man who took the lives of Patricia Docker, Jemima McDonald and Helen Puttock almost forty years before he killed Angelika Kluk? In other words, was Peter Tobin Bible John?

Tobin used two aliases – Pat McLaughlin and James Kelly – before, during and after his murder of Angelika. But as the police delved deeper into this man's very secretive world, they learned that he often called himself not Pat or James but John as he moved around the country. Just as Helen Puttock's killer had.

There are also obvious similarities between the three Bible John victims and Angelika. First, they were all attractive women in their twenties or early thirties. But much more important is the way all four of these women conducted their private lives. Pat, Mima and Helen were all regulars at the Barrowland Ballroom. Bible John thought places like the Barrowland were 'dens of iniquity' that were frequented by 'adulterous' women. He seemed to abhor the fact that married people went there for no-strings-attached one-night stands. Almost forty years later, Angelika slept with a priest and then had an affair with a married man. Tobin probably heard rumours about the affair with Father Nugent and certainly would have known about Martin Macaskill. So what did he think of Angelika's behaviour? Did he feel she needed to be morally 'cleansed' for tainting someone's marriage and luring a man of the cloth into disrepute? If he did, what better way to do so than to murder her and bury her beneath the very church that had given her shelter? Alternatively, the tempta-tion of the young woman he called his 'little apprentice' might simply have been too much for Tobin to resist, regardless of the consequences of an unplanned murder. After all, he made little attempt to conceal his blood-soaked trousers, and his

sudden disappearance from the church made him the prime
suspect almost as soon as the investigation got under way.
Then, when the police caught up with him in London, Tobin
appeared relieved.

Finally, of course, Angelika was murdered right in the heart
of Bible John territory, and Peter Tobin clearly felt comfortable
killing her there. Moreover, scroll back thirty-eight years, and
we find that Tobin was living in Glasgow in 1968, just as Bible
John began to develop his taste for murder.

Chapter Six

Evil-on-Sea: The Margate Murders

Blink and you would have missed it.

The Press Association wire dropped into newsrooms across the country on Monday, 12 November 2007 at 8.46 p.m. It read simply:

> 1 POLICE Missing: Police investigating the disappearance of student Dinah McNicol 16 years ago have found what they think are human remains in a garden in Margate, Kent.

By the early hours of the following morning, the PA was able to elaborate a little:

> 1 POLICE Missing: Detectives investigating the disappearance 16 years ago of a student are examining the 'human remains' found in a garden. Dinah McNicol, of Tillingham, Essex, was 18 when she vanished after attending a music festival in Liphook, Hampshire in August 1991. Police had spent much of yesterday searching the house a

week after announcing that they were reviewing Miss McNicol's disappearance. A spokeswoman said post-mortem tests would be carried out on the remains and the search of the house was continuing, adding: 'It is too early to say whether the remains are those of Dinah McNicol.'

But it would be several more hours before the media knew the whole story. Only once they had been told whose house it was and what had prompted the police to reopen the case into the disappearance of Dinah McNicol did the true magnitude of what was happening in Margate come to light.

Saturday, 3 August 1991

David Tremlett got to his feet and decided to put some distance between himself and the thud of the rave music that was blasting out of the huge sound system. Rave really wasn't his thing, and he was fed up that it had started to creep into the festival scene over the last couple of years. Reggae was more his bag, so it was perhaps inevitable that he would focus on the young girl with braids in her hair among a crowd of thousands. She seemed approachable, so he took the opportunity to say hello. They immediately hit it off, and she quickly introduced herself as Dinah. Chatting about everything and nothing, the eighteen-year-old girl with the pierced nose and the bright green eyes wandered around the festival for the rest of the day with her new friend – browsing among the stalls, checking out the circus and listening to various bands and sound systems pumping out their music.

It had been a good year for festivals, and the Torpedo Town Festival in Liphook, Hampshire, was not bucking the trend.

Posters advertising the free event had been put up everywhere around the M25 – in cafés, bus stops and bars – letting festival-goers know that it would be happening soon. However, to avoid a police ban, the precise details were kept vague. The posters merely proclaimed: 'From Aug 3rd, site to be announced – somewhere in south-east Hampshire.' A few key organisers knew the venue. Everyone else would be told where to go at midday on the 3rd.

By one o'clock, the A3 was already crammed with vehicles heading to Liphook. Bands had signed up, many of them bringing their own stages and PA systems with them, and travellers and ravers alike – who were just starting to mix at the same events – were all making for the same field. Once the police got word of the location, it was far too late – dozens of trucks and coaches were parked up and the festival was well under way. All the officers could do was look on helplessly as a steady stream of people arrived by road and on foot, ready to bed in for the weekend. At the festival's height, more than twenty thousand people were crammed into the Ministry of Defence field that had been chosen for the event.

News of the festival's whereabouts had also reached the local TV stations. Camera crews soon arrived and began filming parents dropping off their children – a sight that was warmly welcomed by the organisers, as it lent a degree of legitimacy to the unauthorised event. Moreover, footage in the evening bulletins showed teenagers enjoying themselves but not getting out of control, which seemed to indicate what a safe environment it was.

For the best part of Saturday and Sunday, David spent his time with Dinah and her friends. They moved between the smaller party gatherings or chilled out in front of the red-and-white-striped Wango Riley stage and in the clearing where Spiral Tribe had set up to the side of the main stage. Dinah was definitely in relaxed mode. She had just completed her A levels at Chelmsford County High School for Girls, so it was time to kick back and enjoy the summer. Why shouldn't she? She'd earned it. She'd worked hard in her five years at the school, and had done well in the exams. There was also the fact that things hadn't been easy over the last few years, since her mother had been killed in a car crash. So she was in the process of making the most of this summer; her promising future and career could wait a few months. Reflecting this, when most of her friends left the festival on the Sunday, Dinah decided to stay on with her new friend for another night. She wouldn't concern herself with how she was going to make the two-and-a-half-hour journey back home until the following day.

On Monday, the pair decided to hitch-hike together, back to their respective homes. After all, they were going in roughly the same direction. They didn't have to wait too long before they got a ride, but it took them only as far as a petrol station further up the A3, just outside the M25. Soon, though, a scruffy man in an old green hatchback pulled up next to the young friends, who were standing by the side of the service station sliproad. David thought the driver seemed a little weird, but he was chatty and friendly towards Dinah.

Perhaps a little too friendly. But he was going their way, and they were both keen to get back home, so they jumped into the car – David in the back and Dinah in the front. David could not hear most of the conversation that took place up front, but he did catch the driver saying something about the Cambridge Folk Festival being much more his style. They explained that David needed to get to Redhill, just half an hour down the road in Surrey, while Dinah's destination was considerably further: Tillingham, in Essex. Junction 8 of the M25 would be great for David – he could even walk from there to his home. But that would mean leavin Dinah on her own with the weird driver, so David suggested that she should come with him. She said she wanted to get home and insisted she would be fine. Nevertheless, David was still anxious as he got out of the car. Something about the driver's attitude just didn't sit right. Even though the man had only just met Dinah, he already seemed over-familiar with her. But Dinah appeared to be completely at ease; and she had earlier given David her phone number, so he would call later to make sure she had arrived home safely. With that, the right-hand indicator flashed and the hatchback slowly edged away. David tried to memorise the licence plate, but the number faded from his mind during his walk home. The image of Dinah's face did not.

'. . . And Please, Don't Have Nightmares. Do Sleep Well. Goodnight'

Just as Nick Ross was giving his regular sign-off at the end of *Crimewatch*, David Tremlett's phone rang. It was a friend, calling to tell him that Dinah McNicol had been featured on the programme and that she had apparently been missing since she and David had parted nine months before. David wasted no time in going to the police in Redhill and telling them that he was the last person to have seen Dinah alive . . . aside from the odd man who had driven her on towards Tillingham. He quickly learned that this was not just a missing person inquiry. It wasn't officially a murder inquiry, yet. But should it turn into one, David had just given the police their first genuine suspect.

Dinah's father had been expecting his daughter home on 5 August. Her no-show was extremely out of character. He knew she could sometimes change her plans, but she would always phone to let him know. Something equally unusual was that money was regularly withdrawn from her building society account after her disappearance. The withdrawals began on 8 August and continued for nearly three weeks, until the account was empty. Each time, the maximum £250 was withdrawn, from cash machines all along the south coast: from Havant, at the most southerly end of the A3, to Hove, Brighton, Portslade, Ramsgate and Margate. Dinah had previously told her family that she might one day use the money to travel, but her passport was still safely stored at home. And she was not the type to blow £2,000 on goods or clothes in a spending spree. In fact, she made many of her own clothes and much of her own jewellery, and did most of her shopping in charity shops.

Despite the *Crimewatch* reconstruction and the information David Tremlett was able to give to the police, the investigation got nowhere. As the months and then the years passed, her family and friends never stopped hoping that she might suddenly appear at the front door. But she never did. And no more information about her disappearance came to light, even though her case was one of the most famous of the early 1990s. So much so that Dinah's photo, along with those of a number of other missing children, formed part of the video that accompanied American rock band Soul Asylum's 1993 hit 'Runaway Train'. As singer Dave Pirner bellows out the song's chorus, Dinah's face appears over the words 'Runaway train, never going back'. Among the other children featured in the video is fifteen-year-old Vicky Hamilton, who also went missing in 1991. Her photo appears at the end of the chorus, over the words: 'Somehow I'm neither here nor there.'

Dinah McNicol was neither here nor there, but she *was* somewhere. Her family only hoped she was alive and well.

Sixteen Years Later – Operation Anagram

Our top story, live at five. The skeleton that could lead to a serial killer. Police fear a convicted sex predator could have murdered at least eleven women going back nearly thirty years after they found human remains at his former home. It's thought that the skeleton is that of Dinah McNicol, who vanished in 1991. Forensic experts are continuing to dig up the back yard of the house in Margate in Kent, once home to Peter Tobin.

Jeremy Thompson, *Live at Five*, Sky News

Although he had just begun a twenty-one-year sentence in the sex offenders' wing at high-security Peterhead Prison for the murder of Angelika Kluk, Peter Tobin had managed to get back into the headlines again. The Press Association wire put it bluntly:

> Officers investigating the disappearance of Dinah McNicol of Tillingham, Essex, 16 years ago, are focusing their inquiries on a previous address of Peter Tobin.

During the investigation into the murder of Angelika Kluk, detectives had built up and analysed a comprehensive timeline of Tobin's life. He had travelled extensively throughout the country, but detectives had eventually been able to establish his known associates and, crucially, where he had lived. Senior officers from forty-three forces across the country with outstanding missing persons inquiries were invited to a summit with the intention of plotting the killer's movements over the last forty years. The whole process was given the code name Operation Anagram. It was set up on the assumption that Tobin had almost certainly killed before, possibly many times.

Operation Anagram made an early breakthrough when it discovered that Tobin was living in the town of Bathgate when Vicky Hamilton went missing in February 1991. Strathclyde Police searched every inch of Tobin's former home in Robertson Avenue, including squeezing through the narrow ceiling hatch to gain access to the loft space. There, carefully concealed in the rafters, they found a knife. On that knife, they found a tiny fragment of Vicky Hamilton's skin.

Of course, the officers involved in Operation Anagram were well aware that another teenager had gone missing in 1991. But Dinah McNicol had vanished after being picked up in Hampshire, a very long way from central Scotland. Before long, though, detectives discovered that Tobin had moved to Margate, on the Kent coast, after the disappearance of Vicky but before Dinah went missing. That put him closer, but still some distance from Hampshire. Then it emerged that Tobin's estranged wife and their son Daniel were living near Portsmouth in 1991. Having been granted access to his son, Tobin would regularly make the drive to and from Margate, especially at the weekend. His route would take him up and down the M25 and the A3. There was also the fact that Dinah's cash card had been used in both Margate and Havant, just five miles from Portsmouth, in the weeks following her disappearance.

The police started to accumulate dozens of items of women's jewellery, collected from Tobin's previous addresses, and began to fear the worst. Were these trophies he had collected over the years from numerous other victims? The detectives knew what they had to do: they had to look Peter Tobin straight in the eye and ask him a few simple questions.

On 21 July 2007, a few weeks after his conviction for the murder of Angelika Kluk, Tobin was duly interviewed at Frazerburgh Police Station. With one knee on the chair and his other foot flat on the floor as he rested both palms on the table, Tobin was quizzed by two officers for information about the disappearance of Vicky Hamilton. Detective Constable David Crookston showed Tobin a photograph of the girl:

Tobin: Don't know her.

Officer: Have you got anything to say about the girl's disappearance?

Tobin: Nothing at all, don't know nothing.

Officer: You've never met Vicky?

Tobin: Not to my knowledge, no. I don't even know if I sat next to her on a bus, or whatever, a train, you know what I mean.

Officer: Is there any way that you can assist us in finding this girl now?

Tobin: No.

Officer: Her parents don't know, or her father doesn't know, where she is. Her family, we, don't know—

Tobin: Sorry I can nae help ye. As I say, I've never met her . . . I've never . . . never . . .

Officer: You have no knowledge where—?

Tobin: No.

Dogged Determination

Tobin's lack of cooperation meant police forces had to follow up every lead or apparent coincidence, just in case it proved to be significant. But Vicky and Dinah remained top of their list. Investigators managed to establish precisely where Tobin had been living in the summer of 1991, and the house in Margate became the focus of Essex Police's investigation. The force's Investigative Review Team drafted in a number of detectives from the Major Investigation Section to help with the inquiry. They hoped that a fresh appeal might generate some information, so Detective Superintendent

Tim Wills, the officer in charge of the investigation, told reporters:

> The disappearance of Dinah has remained a mystery for too many years and Essex Police will always look at new opportunities to solve such mysteries. Dinah was an intelligent and vibrant young woman who had her whole life ahead of her. I would love to believe that she is out there somewhere living that life, but I would not be doing my job if I did not investigate the possibility that someone may have harmed her in some way. No family should have to live so many years not knowing what has happened to someone they love, and if we can take advantage of science, technology and even changes in allegiances to bring this family answers, then we will. I know a lot of years have passed but it makes this disappearance no less important and I want to hear from anyone who remembers the disappearance and has any information that might be useful to us. No matter how irrelevant the information may seem, I want to know about it. It may just be the piece of the jigsaw that we need to finally solve this case.

Rude Awakening

Nicola Downing and her boyfriend Mark Drage were startled by the knock on their front door – they had not been expecting anyone. The couple and Ms Downing's four children had lived peacefully at 50 Irvine Drive, Margate, for twelve years. But their visitors on Friday, 9 November 2007 were about to disturb that peace in the most abrupt and invasive way. The family would be obliged to pack suitcases, move into a local hotel, and then watch as their modest three-bedroom home was turned upside down, its contents removed and gardens dug up, before possibly being dismantled brick by brick. They would even be expected to help – by informing detectives of any alterations they had made to the house. All of this was necessary because of events that had happened sixteen years ago and had nothing to do with them.

And if that wasn't shocking enough, it took the twenty-strong forensics team little more than twelve hours, once the search had begun in earnest two days later, to reveal the horror that had lain only inches beneath the family's feet throughout their time in the terraced house.

Three forensic archaeologists armed with ground-penetrating radar (GPR) equipment were able to identify soil that had been disturbed in any way. A series of electrical pulses sent into the ground in the thirty-foot back garden allowed the investigators to map where anything might have been concealed below the surface. The equipment saved officers a great deal of time, and to some extent made up for Tobin's unwillingness to help with the investigation. Having analysed their results, the forensic archaeologists began digging in a specific area of the garden, next to the shed. Just below the turf, they came across a layer of concrete and chalk. Carefully, they broke through the tough layers to find out what lay beneath. It soon transpired that they had discovered a makeshift grave. Inside there were two separate bundles, each wrapped in a black plastic bag, placed beside one another, and entangled by roots. One of the bags had been pierced by a root, which allowed the officers to see that it contained more black and green plastic bags.

Further investigation revealed that the two outer bin-liners contained body parts that had been individually wrapped in the inner bags. The forensics team quickly established that they were dealing with a woman's body that had been cut in half at the abdomen. The hands and arms were crossed over in front of the woman's face, while the lower half had been placed in a kneeling position. Both body sections had been bound. Having been placed into body bags, the packages were exhumed by Essex Police for closer examination. They hoped two rings found on the hands of the victim would help to identify her. They also found lengths of cord, a sweatshirt, a red polo shirt and a white bra.

That evening, from his family home in Tillingham, Dinah's father, Ian McNicol, gave his first response to the discovery: 'Ninety-nine per cent of me thinks she has been murdered, but there is just that one per cent that doesn't know. I want to die in peace, knowing what happened to my daughter.'

Over the weekend, the media began to run with the story. Once the name 'Peter Tobin' and his gruesome killing ways had been conclusively linked to the Margate house, editors started to speculate that the discovery of one body might lead to another, then another. There were suggestions that the house would reveal Tobin's full 'back catalogue' of crimes. Predictably, 50 Irvine Drive was soon dubbed a 'house of horrors'. Police had already told journalists that Tobin was now a suspect in at least twelve unsolved murders, which naturally generated comparisons with Fred and Rose West and their house in Cromwell Street, Gloucester. The nickname 'Bible John' was also starting to be uttered in connection with Tobin.

By the time the television cameras rolled into Irvine Drive, though, the coroner's ambulance had already taken away the woman's skeletal remains for a post-mortem examination. But everyone, not least Ian McNicol, would have to wait for confirmation that the body was indeed that of his daughter. In an attempt to appease the burgeoning and increasingly inquisitive press pack that had entrenched itself along the normally quiet residential street, an Essex Police spokeswoman delivered a short statement to reporters: 'It has not been possible at this stage to establish cause of death or ascertain age or time of death. It is too early to say whether the remains are those of Dinah McNicol. It may be some days before we are able formally to say whether it is or not. However, as well as human remains, some personal effects were discovered.'

Taking advantage of the renewed interest in the case, and perhaps sympathetically pandering to Ian McNicol's '1 per cent' chance that his daughter might still be alive, the police issued a new photo of Dinah in an effort to jog the memories of any witnesses to her disappearance. It showed a distinctly more relaxed young woman compared to the image that had been used ever since the initial investigation had begun. Another new image was widely publicised at this point, too. Through police channels, the Missing People charity released an age-progressed image that showed how Dinah might look at the age of thirty-four. Like everyone else, the charity hoped that the investigation would end sixteen years of heartache for the McNicol family and their friends.

On Wednesday, 14 November, the police search of 50 Irvine Drive resumed in the early hours of the morning. Most of the rear garden had by now been dug up and the soil shovelled into more than a dozen large waste bins, ready to be analysed later in greater detail. The full shock of what had been discovered in the back garden had begun to sink in, especially for those who had known Peter Tobin when he had lived in the house. He was widely described as a regular guy who appeared quite normal. David Martin described him as an ideal neighbour: 'The first thing you realise about Peter Tobin is how normal he is. He's not something that crawls out of the woodwork even if that's what appears at a later stage. No, he's absolutely normal – like talking to your best mate or someone down the pub.'

Not everyone felt the same way about their former neighbour, though. Now in her twenties, Laura Harris remembered Tobin as 'creepy': 'He can't have been living in the house any longer than two years. I remember talking to him. The scary part of it was he offered to babysit me and my sister when we were younger. My mum wasn't having any of it because we didn't know him.'

The peace of the suburban street had been well and truly shattered by the police and media presence. Aside from the grim secrets that were being unearthed, not everyone welcomed the satellite vans and cherry-pickers, brought in to help cameras get a better vantage point from which to film the ongoing search of the garden. One young entrepreneur even began offering access to his bedroom, which overlooked the garden, at £10 a pop. But the gradual appearance of bouquets – geraniums and roses – against the wall in an area roped off by the police reminded everyone of the human tragedy that was unfolding on their doorstep. And it was about to get worse.

By mid-morning on the 14th, rumours had started to spread

through the press pack that perhaps the remains were not those of Dinah McNicol. Before long, Tim Wills appeared to make a statement: 'When the body was examined at the mortuary there were personal effects on the body that would lead me to think that it probably isn't Dinah McNicol. I'm waiting for scientific confirmation which could be some days away. At this time, I don't believe it is Dinah McNicol.'

The police had known what clothes and jewellery Dinah had been wearing on the day she'd disappeared. But not one of those items had been unearthed in the garden. It therefore seemed undeniable that the police had found a different victim altogether. This was a huge blow for Dinah's father, who had been almost certain that he was about to be able to close the book on sixteen years of misery. Nevertheless, the sixty-eight-year-old was stoic when he talked to the press:

It's another poor girl. They found bits of clothing and they were able to confirm it was not Dinah. My family hoped it was Dinah so we could put her to rest and go through our grieving process, but obviously we can't now. But it's not finished. They are looking to see if it's another Fred West – if there are more bodies there. They thought Dinah may be there because her cash card was used in Margate. This is obviously a setback for us but, after 16, almost 17, years, I'm keeping my fingers crossed they will find her.

By lunchtime, a new rumour had started to spread: the police had positively identified the victim. At the mortuary in Margate, forensic ondontologist Geoffrey Moody had checked the victim's teeth pattern with the dental records of several missing girls. At 2 p.m., an announcement was made outside the Irvine Drive address. It confirmed what the press pack already suspected: 'Lothian and Borders Police can confirm that the body found in the house in Margate, Kent, on 12 November is that of Vicky Hamilton. A man arrested in July 2007 has been charged in connection with the disappearance of Vicky Hamilton and a report submitted to the Procurator Fiscal.'

Everyone gathered in the street knew precisely who that 'man' was. In Peterhead Prison, Peter Tobin had just been arrested on suspicion of the murder of Vicky Hamilton.

Sixteen Years Earlier

The machine spat out the Eastern Scottish bus ticket. Printed on it was the date – 10 February 1991 – and the time – 16.59. They had just made it. The thick snow crunched underfoot as Vicky Hamilton leaned into a tight farewell hug with her sister at the bus stop. It was the first time Vicky had stayed with her older sister Sharon in Livingston. They had had such a fun time together that they had already made plans for her to return the following weekend.

'Tell me which buses again,' Vicky asked her sister.

Sharon repeated where and when Vicky would have to change buses along her route, until she was sure her little sister knew exactly what to do. But she could still sense that Vicky was nervous about the fifteen-mile journey to their mum's place in Redding. They had checked with the bus company that the routes were still running despite the heavy snowfall. Vicky was glad that they were because, despite a great weekend, she was keen to get home to watch a music awards ceremony on television that evening.

'Can you tell my sister where she needs to get off to catch her next bus?' Sharon asked the driver of the 281 Edinburgh-to-Bathgate service, keen for Vicky to get some help once she'd departed Livingston. The driver said he would. At 17.05 on the dot, the bus pulled away with each sister waving goodbye.

Vicky sat back in her seat. In spite of her sister's detailed instructions, and the knowledge that the driver would help, she could not have been confident about making the journey with no problems. After all, on her way to Sharon's two days earlier, she had become confused at one of her scheduled changes in Linlithgow and had been forced to ask a stranger to point her in the direction of the bus to Bathgate. A friendly woman in her twenties called Elspeth Kenny had helped her out and, even better, told Vicky she was going all the way to Livingston, too. Vicky had been so excited about her visit that she told her travel companion all about her family and how much she was looking forward to a night out with her big sister. In fact, she had done most of the talking all the way to Bathgate, where the bus pulled over to let them off. With the snow getting worse, Elspeth had insisted that they should take a taxi the final few miles to Livingston. Before Vicky got out at Sharon's, she had assured her new friend that if it was still snowing on Sunday, her Dad would come and collect her.

The sisters had spent the whole of Friday night catching up on each other's news, which had led to a long lie-in on Saturday morning. Once up, they had spent much of the day shopping in Livingston town centre before going out with a group of Sharon's friends that evening. Vicky had fitted in well with the older girls, and had made everyone laugh.

But with the weekend over all too soon, Vicky had packed up her holdall, placed her purse and other valuables in a shoulder bag and checked she had all her jewellery – a ring with a reddish stone and heart-shaped signet ring. (The rings weren't actually Vicky's. She had raided her mother's jewellery box before leaving, as she always did.) Slipping on her black bomber jacket, Unisys sweatshirt and brown Hushpuppies, Vicky and Sharon had then headed for the bus stop.

Vicky had done a lot of growing up over the last few months. For instance, she had experienced the anxiety of a pregnancy test at the doctor's. She was starting to assert her independence. So while she had the option of calling her dad for a lift, it seems that she was determined to make the trip by public transport. After about twenty minutes, the 281 pulled into Bathgate's King Street – that wasn't where the bus had stopped on Friday. And because she had been chatting with Elspeth that day, and the two of them had then taken a taxi, she hadn't made a note of the stop for the next bus she needed to catch – to Falkirk. As promised, the driver had told Vicky where to get off, but she had not thought to ask him where to go for her connection. She was left standing alone in the street with her two bags.

'Excuse me, excuse me, please. Can you tell me the time and the place for the bus to Falkirk?' Vicky politely asked a man in his late thirties, stopping him in his tracks.

The man looked up from his bag of chips and thought for a second. He had been at a local bar having a few drinks before hunger had struck. 'I think this is where you need to be, but

I'm not sure what time it stops here. Sorry,' he replied.

Helpful, but Vicky wanted to be certain. So, with the little loose change she had on her, she decided to get herself a bag at the shop just over the road.

'Here you go,' the lady behind the counter said as she passed Vicky her chips.

'Do you know where I go to get the bus to Falkirk,' asked Vicky as she paid.

'Straight down the street across from the police station. It's just a couple of minutes' walk away,' replied the lady. 'It's the blue bus. You can get it on the hour, and they come about every hour,' she added.

With that, Vicky left the shop and stepped back out into the cold February evening. She darted across the road just as the lights changed. The first car had already begun to pull away and was forced to break suddenly, stopping just in time on the slippery road surface. Startled, Vicky glanced briefly at the driver, as if to acknowledge that she was in the wrong, and then hastily reached the kerb on the other side of the road.

She then paused for a few minutes in an area the locals knew as the 'Steelyard', sitting on a bench to eat her chips. She was just a hundred metres or so from the correct bus stop, and after a few minutes she started to walk towards it. A man on his way to the video store confirmed that she was going in the right direction, although he added that he didn't know when the next bus was due.

What happened over the next few minutes of Vicky Hamilton's life is unclear. Several witnesses saw her waiting alone at the bus stop, but she never boarded the bus to Falkirk. Given the help she'd received from Elspeth Kenny on her outward journey, it's entirely possible that Vicky reacted with relief rather than suspicion when she was approached by another stranger who seemed keen to help her reach her destination safely. Tragically, though, this time, that stranger was Peter Tobin.

As we have seen, Tobin has never even admitted that he met Vicky Hamilton, let alone confessed to her murder, so we can only speculate about how he abducted her. His home in Robertson Avenue was just around the corner from the bus stop, so maybe he told Vicky she could phone her father and organise a lift home from there. Maybe he pulled over in his own car – perhaps with his visiting son in the back in a baby seat, which would have demonstrated his trustworthiness – and offered her a lift all the way back to Redding. Maybe he offered her a warm drink laced with a sedative. Maybe he simply grabbed her violently off the pavement and bundled her into his car.

What we do know is that ten minutes after Vicky had arrived at the bus stop, the bus from Bathgate to Falkirk pulled into the side of the road and she was no longer waiting there.

Hide and Seek

Soon the police were scouring Bathgate, looking for Vicky Hamilton. The story of the missing girl had been all over the newspapers and TV, and officers were asking a lot of people a lot of questions. But the police did not talk to Peter Tobin. He hadn't been in the area long, and he kept himself to himself. He said hello to his neighbours on the rare occasions he saw them in the street, but that was it. He did a few odd jobs for people, such as fixing cars, but nothing permanent. He preferred it that way: keep under the radar, keep a low profile. He had good reason. He was the only person who knew what had happened to Vicky Hamilton, and he would do everything in his power to stop his dark secret coming out.

The pebble-dashed, council-owned 11 Robertson Avenue was in a quiet, secluded part of Bathgate. The dead-end street became home to Tobin, his wife Cathy Wilson and their son Daniel when they moved up from Brighton in September 1989. But Cathy left the next year and moved to Hampshire, taking Daniel with her. Not long after, Tobin was admitted to hospital in West Lothian after taking an overdose of the anti-depressant amitriptyline and triazolam, which is used to relieve anxiety. He told the doctors he'd tried to take his own life because he'd been left by his family. Now he lived a solitary existence.

We do not know for certain what Tobin did with Vicky's body in the immediate aftermath of killing her. He might have deposited her in the boot of his car or in the back of a van. But a visit from an electrician in the days following the abduction leads us to believe that he hid her in a cupboard under the stairs. Tobin seems to have forgotten all about the scheduled rewiring of his home and the fact that he had been instructed to clear the cupboard, which was where the work needed to be done. Once the electrician had insisted on entering the house, Tobin repeatedly told him that he could not allow access to the under-stairs space that day. 'Oh, you cunt!' the electrician exclaimed as he ignored Tobin's protestations and opened the cupboard door to discover the space still packed with bags and boxes. The comment gave Tobin a way out of a possibly perilous situation: he reacted angrily to the electrician's expletive, making out that it was directed at him, and an argument ensued. To Tobin's relief, the electrician left quickly, complaining of threatening behaviour, and he didn't return the next day. That probably gave Tobin the time he needed to find a better hiding-place for the body. When Cathy came to visit a couple of days later to collect Daniel, who had been staying with Tobin over the weekend, he was much calmer.

However, the intense police investigation may well have affected his health. On 22 February, twelve days after he murdered Vicky, Tobin was treated at St John's Hospital for acute abdominal pain. The previous day, he had done something extremely risky in a bid to send the police off on a false trail, so maybe the pain he felt was caused by anxiety.

Either by design or circumstance, Tobin was in St Andrew Square, Edinburgh, on 21 February. In his possession was Vicky Hamilton's purse. Inside was the bus ticket she had purchased on the 10th, as well as a London address, scrawled on a piece of paper; a leaflet about oral contraception; an appointment card for Falkirk and District Royal Infirmary; a letter from a friend; Vicky's identity card; a star-sign card for Taurus with 'Vicky Hamilton OK' written on the back; a money-off voucher for cigarettes; another scrap of paper with several names and numbers; a note to be excused from school for a dental appointment; two cards with the phrases 'If music be the food of love' and 'Kisses are good for you, especially mine' printed on them; and a piece of paper with the word 'Samaritans' and a telephone number.

It was raining as Tobin sidled up to a large yellow portable cabin, set up temporarily on a corner of the square as part of a construction project. Taking the purse out of his pocket, he tossed it into some leaves, close to the pavement edge, so it was still clearly visible to the naked eye. Presumably his intention was to get the police thinking that Vicky had passed through Edinburgh en route to somewhere else. And with the city's extensive transport links, that could mean anywhere in the country. If the police took the bait, the focus would shift well away from Bathgate.

Probably before Tobin had even left the city centre, the purse was spotted by a passer-by and handed in to the police. It was barely wet, so the police realised that it could not have been lying on the pavement for very long. Within days, Lothian and Borders Police had returned Vicky's purse to her family in Redding, sparking renewed hope that she was still alive.

Because the purse was found so close to Edinburgh's bus and railway stations, the police did indeed begin to widen their enquiries, taking in cities from Aberdeen in the north to London in the south. They would eventually speak to more than 6,500 people and take more than 3,000 statements in the first year alone. Tobin's risky plan had paid off.

But it was still time for him to move on. He was never one to stay in one place for long anyway. Now it was all about covering his tracks and seeking somewhere to lie low for a while. He'd already ensured the knife was in a safe place. That had been a top priority, as he'd used it to slice up his young victim in order to make her transportation more manageable. He'd placed the eleven-inch blade between the masonry and the last wooden joist in the loft, behind three old bell jars, and at least five metres from the small access hatch. Even if some future tenant were to have a good snoop around up there, they would be hard pressed to find it.

Tobin needed to put some real distance between himself and Bathgate. He got in touch with Scottish Homes, his land-lords, and made a request for a council house swap. He explained that his wife and son were now living on the south coast, so a move in that general direction would be appreci-ated. He was lucky. Soon he was contacted and told that a couple from Margate had expressed a desire to move to Scotland. The housing exchange between Tobin and Peter and Hannah Hewitson was given the go-ahead by all the rel-evant authorities and the date for the exchange was set for 22 March.

On the day itself, Tobin wasted no time leaving 11 Robert-son Avenue. He asked his neighbour at number 14, Kevin Ellis, if he would look after some belongings for a couple of weeks until Tobin could come back and collect them. There simply wasn't enough room in the back of the van for everything. Kevin agreed and Tobin handed over some motorbike equip-ment and several demijohn bottles. With that, he was gone. He left the Bathgate house in such a state that the Hewitsons had to spend days cleaning and bleaching the inside of the property, just to get rid of the stench. They thought it smelled almost as if someone had died at 11 Robertson Avenue.

In the back of Tobin's van was his secret cargo – the dis-membered body of Vicky Hamilton. He would decide what to do with her once he arrived at his new home – 50 Irvine Drive, Margate.

15 November 2007

The searches continued in the garden of 50 Irvine Drive. Now perhaps more than ever, the police were sure that they would find the body of Dinah McNicol at the seaside terrace. Meanwhile, five hundred miles away, a sixteen-year wait was finally coming to an end for Vicky Hamilton's father: the man accused of his daughter's murder was about to be escorted into the dock.

A few members of the public had gathered on the street outside Linlithgow Sheriff Court to see what all the media attention was about – who was being brought to court. As the prison van turned into the street leading up to the court building, Michael Hamilton stepped into the middle of the road. Then, alongside a police officer, he slowly and sombrely began to lead the van to the court gates. Head slightly bowed, hands in jacket pockets, not uttering a word, trying hard to hide the emotion and hatred he felt towards the man who was sitting handcuffed behind the blacked-out windows just yards away from him. Michael had fought to keep his daughter's case in the public eye and was determined to see that justice was eventually done.

A spokesman for the Crown Office made a statement: 'Peter Britton Tobin, aged sixty-one, today appeared in private, on petition, at Linlithgow Sheriff Court. He has been charged with the murder of Vicky Hamilton. He made no plea or declaration, he was detained for further examination, and he remains in custody.'

After the brief appearance behind the closed doors of Courtroom 2, Tobin was led back to the van through the rear door of the court to be transported back to prison to continue his life sentence for the murder of Angelika Kluk. When the van reappeared, years of pent-up anger and frustration finally erupted in Michael Hamilton. Standing in the street alongside his two brothers, his sister-in-law and more than fifty other people, he had to be restrained by police as he hammered on the side of the van and hurled abuse at Tobin.

It was left to Vicky's uncle, Eric Hamilton, to make an understandably brief statement: 'All I can say is that Mike is happy the long road is nearly at an end. We just want peace and to put Vicky where she belongs.'

Tobin had not yet been found guilty, although the circumstantial evidence appeared overwhelming. He was in Bathgate on the day Vicky disappeared. A neighbour had even seen him out in the town that very evening, just hours after Vicky had gone missing, probably having left her dead or dying back at his home. Tobin had a history of violent sexual attacks against teenage girls. And, of course, he had lived in the house in Margate where Vicky's body was finally found.

All of these pieces of evidence, especially the last one, were compelling. But they *were* circumstantial, and might not be sufficient to convict Tobin. This is where advanced DNA technology came in to play the crucial role.

Child's Play

Operation Anagram's research into Peter Tobin and his itinerant lifestyle in the aftermath of his arrest for the murder of Angelika Kluk in 2006 was crucial in uncovering his connection with Bathgate and therefore his link to the disappearance of Vicky Hamilton. And the horrendous injuries sustained by the Polish student gave the police a graphic indication of what Tobin was capable of doing. But it was only through analysis of the knife found in the loft of 11 Robertson Avenue that the true extent of Tobin's evil was revealed. It yielded incontrovertible proof that Tobin was directly linked to Vicky's death, especially after he admitted in court (much to the prosecution's amazement) that the knife was 'probably' his. Forensic scientists had discovered a tiny fragment of what appeared to be skin on the underside of the knife. From this they managed to obtain a partial DNA profile that matched Vicky's. The chance of the fragment of skin coming from anyone other than Vicky was one in a million.

But the police needed yet more evidence before they could be confident of convincing a jury that Tobin had taken the young girl's life. Throughout the sixteen years of the inquiry, naturally the police had assumed that, if Vicky had indeed been killed, her body would have been hidden somewhere in or around Bathgate. They had not reckoned on it being dissected to make its transportation easier, and then driven five hundred miles to Margate. But that is precisely what Tobin did. Vicky was literally cut in half at the waist. Then Tobin placed the legs and lower abdomen in one plastic bin-liner, and the torso, arms and head in another. He then casually loaded the bags into the van he was using for his move along with his personal belongings, many of which were similarly packaged. But while he was careful not to do anything that would arouse suspicion as he moved out of Robertson Avenue, he left other clues that would come back to haunt him sixteen years later.

The first breakthrough came when police scientists examined the bag that had contained Vicky's torso. The plastic surface yielded four fingerprints, all of which matched those of Peter Tobin: two from his left ring finger, one from his right middle finger and one from his right little finger. Clearly, at some point, Tobin had forgotten to wear gloves when lifting the bag.

The second crucial piece of evidence that came to light after Vicky's body was found came in the form of more DNA. During the post-mortem examination, the pathologist took two 'intimate' swabs and found traces of what was probably semen. The samples matched Tobin's DNA profile, with the chance of them not coming from him being one in 34,000.

Closer examination of Vicky's body also helped the police understand how Tobin had managed to subdue and kill his victim. Bruising to the fifteen-year-old's hand, chest, back and neck suggested that she had been involved in a violent incident just before her death. The bruising on her hand stemmed from her attempts to defend herself from the attack. The injuries on the rest of her body were probably sustained by being forced to the floor, where she was raped and strangled.

One thing the police could not know was whether Tobin deliberately went out that night looking for prey. More likely, he seized an unexpected opportunity to put into practice a fantasy that had been running through his mind for some time. The most plausible scenario is that he lured Vicky back to his house, then somehow managed to convince her to come inside. But sooner or later he would have to subdue her if he were to carry out what he had now committed himself to do. Toxicological test results gave a strong indication of how he managed to do that. Traces of amitriptyline were found in Vicky's liver, suggesting that she swallowed the drug shortly before her death. At Tobin's trial, the jury was told that the antidepressant is a strong sedative which lowers the heart rate. And, of course, we know that Tobin was admitted to hospital after taking an overdose of amitriptyline in 1990, so he was well aware of its power and could well have had a stock of it in the house.

Tobin probably thought that he had committed the perfect murder. No one in Bathgate or Margate really knew who he was, and he had moved from one end of Britain to the other in a quite commonplace council house swap, distancing himself from what, at the time, was still only a missing person inquiry. He had even led the police on a merry dance by leaving Vicky's purse for them to find in Edinburgh, a ploy that had seriously hampered the initial investigation. But what Tobin must have thought was a masterstroke would eventually become one of his biggest mistakes.

When the purse was analysed sixteen years after it had been handed back to Vicky's family, traces of DNA were found all over it. The samples did not match Peter Tobin's DNA profile, but they did match his son's. It was concluded that Tobin either gave the purse to three-year-old Daniel to play with or Daniel simply got his hands on it himself. Then, as most infants do, he placed it in his mouth and covered it with saliva.

The evidence, especially that acquired by scientific advances that had occurred since Vicky Hamilton's death, was becoming irrefutable.

16 November 2007

At 1.50 p.m., the news wire confirmed what everyone had expected to hear sooner or later:

1 POLICE Missing: Essex Police who are searching convicted paedophile Peter Tobin's former home in Margate today found a second body.

Within a couple hours, the coroner's ambulance was loaded with another victim, identity as yet unknown. It didn't remain a mystery for long. Assistant Chief Constable of Essex Police Peter Lowton told reporters that the new body's height, clothing and jewellery were all consistent with it being that of Dinah McNicol. Once again, her father Ian spoke to the press: 'It has been a long wait. The one per cent has now gone. We can actually have her remains, put her remains next to her mother's, actually have time to mourn and get on with life. I always said I wanted to know what happened to my daughter before I died. At least I can now die in peace.'

However, it's hard to believe that Mr McNicol truly found peace once the horrific nature of his daughter's murder was revealed. As they had with Vicky Hamilton, the Forensic Science Service found traces of amitriptyline in Dinah McNicol's body. The drug would have caused her to feel drowsy and dizzy. It would also have made it difficult for her to fight back when Tobin attempted to rape her. When officers opened the bag containing Dinah's body, they discovered she was partially clothed – in a green jacket and a dark sleeveless vest. Her watch was still on her wrist, a necklace was round her neck, and her nose ring remained in place. But her green trousers and knickers had been pushed down over her buttocks, suggesting that a sexual assault had been attempted. Later, a Home Office pathologist concluded that Dinah's death was consistent with ligature strangulation and gagging. Rather than being cut in half, like Vicky Hamilton, Dinah had been bent double. A ligature around her head had been fastened to a clothes-line ligature around her ankles. A third ligature had been tied around her right thigh then fastened to her right wrist before passing around her back to repeat the process on her left side. A fourth had been placed around her neck, and a knotted gag had been placed in her mouth. The bags in which the body had been wrapped were examined for fingerprints. Three thumb-prints and one fingerprint were discovered not only on the bags but on the tape that had been used to seal them. All belonged to Tobin.

When Peter Tobin was eventually tried for the murder of Dinah McNicol at Chelmsford Crown Court in December 2009, the jury was told that in order to conceal the fact that he was digging a grave in his garden, the defendant had made up a cover story. At one point, Tobin's neighbour David Martin had peered over his garden fence to see Tobin waist deep in a hole with a shovel in his hand. Mr Martin had thought the sight was funny and had asked if Tobin was attempting to dig to Australia. Tobin had continued the joke, adding that it was better than paying the ten-pound fare. He had then said he was actually digging a sandpit for his son, who came to visit at weekends. But some days later, the hole had been filled in. Prosecutor William Clegg, QC explained to the court that Tobin had subsequently told his neighbour that a visit from Social Services had deemed the sandpit too dangerous. In reality, of course, there had been no such visit.

Peter Tobin chose not to take the stand in his trial for the murder of Dinah McNicol, and communicated solely through his lawyer. In fact, on his instruction, no defence whatsoever was presented. However, he did plead not guilty, so the prosecution still had to prove that he was responsible for Dinah's death. That was not too difficult a task. In an unusual turn of events, the jury was told on day one that Peter Tobin was a convicted paedophile who had already begun a life sentence for the murder of Vicky Hamilton, whose body had been found just yards away from Dinah's in the same garden in Margate. Just in case the jury was toying with the idea that this might be some kind of astonishing coincidence, William Clegg concluded his closing statement by saying: 'Did a stranger arrive at 50 Irvine Drive to find that the occupier had conveniently dug a hole and then dumped her [Dinah's] body in it? And of all the gardens in the South-East of England, the murderer of Dinah McNicol happens to select the garden of another murderer who had already buried his victim there? If this were not so serious, it would be ludicrous!'

It took more than eighteen years for Tobin to be brought to trial for the murder of Dinah McNicol, but just thirteen minutes for the jury to reach its guilty verdict. Tobin's convictions in the cases of Vicky Hamilton and Dinah McNicol, added to that for his murder of Angelika Kluk, made the sixty-two-year-old Britain's latest serial killer. But there were still gaps in the police's knowledge of where Tobin had been and what he had done throughout his life. Which meant there were almost certainly more of his victims waiting to be discovered.

Bible John – Just More Violent?

The similarities between the three Bible John murders and Peter Tobin's murders of Vicky Hamilton, Dinah McNicol and Angelika Kluk are considerable. The most glaring is that all six women were killed in the same way. Bible John strangled his three victims – Mima McDonald and Helen Puttock with their own stockings. Mima and Helen were also partially clothed when they were discovered, and there had been a degree of sexual activity either prior to or after their deaths. Similarly, Vicky and Dinah were strangled, with Dinah's own clothes used against her during Tobin's attack – her ankles were tied with her headscarf, and her leggings were used to bind her wrists. Leggings for Tobin; stockings for Bible John. Angelika, Vicky and Dinah were also sexually abused.

At first glance, though, there seems to be a disparity between the level of violence employed by Bible John in the late 1960s and that displayed by Tobin in 1991 and 2006. However, it should be remembered that Bible John was much more violent when he killed for the third time than he had been when murdering Pat and Mima: Helen was savagely beaten and there was blood all over her face when she was found. It is therefore reasonable to suggest that, if Bible John did indeed continue to kill, his level of violence would have escalated with each attack – if only to satisfy his increasingly lurid fantasies.

There are further similarities in the car journeys undertaken with their killer by Helen and Dinah – the former in a taxi, the latter as a hitch-hiker. In each case a third party had to be dealt with before the murderer could achieve his goal, but on both occasions this was a fairly straightforward task. Bible John instructed the taxi driver to drop off Jeannie first, so she would not be left alone in the cab. Twenty-two years later, Tobin picked up Dinah knowing that her friend – David Tremlett – would have to leave the car first. And just as Bible John was charming and gallant towards Helen in the taxi, Tobin worked hard to put Dinah at ease and make her feel comfortable in his car. Consequently, neither woman had any qualms about being taken home alone by the man who would eventually kill her.

Finally, we might look at a specific comment made in the taxi and another made in the green hatchback. Bible John said he liked golf rather than football. Peter Tobin said he preferred the Cambridge Folk Festival to the type of event that his two young passengers had just attended. The subtle implication being made by both Bible John and Tobin was that they were (or he was) of a somewhat higher class than the other people in the car.

Chapter Seven

Policing Homicide – Science and Clairvoyance

> He felt the girl's clothing, which showed dried blood, received an immediate impression, sighed, pointed to a spot on the map which was included in the package and dictated into the tape recorder: 'This girl was beaten and murdered here where I marked an "X".' He described her murder in detail and gave some clues about the murderer which helped the police apprehend him.
>
> Jack Harrison Pollack describing a case undertaken by the clairvoyant Gerard Croiset (1964)

Since 1968, there have been a number of developments in how a murder is investigated and the perpetrator apprehended. In particular, extensive use is now made of forensic science and a growing range of experts, including profilers. Whereas fingerprints were probably the greatest weapon in the arsenal of detectives in 1968, nowadays tiny fragments of hair, fibres, semen and blood can help identify a suspect and lead to an arrest. So great has been the development of forensic science that so-called cold murder cases – those that remain unsolved, possibly after decades – are now being re-investigated using techniques that had not been dreamed of when these crimes were committed. In some instances, the police might have collected the evidence but simply had no means of analysing it at the time. However, as long as that evidence is stored correctly, a new technique might always be developed to reveal the information it contains.

Many of us think we know all about forensic science through watching TV dramas and documentaries. But to what extent do those programmes reflect the reality of how British police currently attempt to solve cold cases?

'Forensic' simply means of (or used in) a court of law, so 'forensic science' is the application of scientific – usually medical – knowledge to a legal issue. Back in 1968–9, when the police were investigating the murders of Pat Docker, Mima McDonald and Helen Puttock, they employed methods and techniques – and sometimes experts – that dated back to the early days of forensic science, which was pioneered in Home Office laboratories in the 1930s. It was then that the country's police forces first received Forensic Science Circulars that emphasised the importance of science as a tool that should be utilised in crime detection. In response, the Metropolitan Police established the first specialist, large-scale laboratory in 1935, and under Home Office guidance others were opened in Nottingham in 1936 and Birmingham and Cardiff in 1938.

These early developments in forensic science should not disguise the reality that the field was dominated by a handful of qualified practitioners – most notably Sir Bernard Spilsbury and Professor Keith Simpson south of the border, and Professor Sydney Smith in Scotland. Moreover, there was little love lost between these three men and their supporters, so there was no pooling of their ideas and techniques – each went in a direction that suited his own tastes and interests. Smith, from Edinburgh University, wrote the classic textbook *Forensic Medicine and Toxicology*, published in 1925, and he crossed swords with Spilsbury during the trial of Sidney Fox for the murder of his mother in 1930. Spilsbury – acting for the Crown – insisted that Mrs Fox had been strangled by her son, a conclusion he had reached after examining a bruise on her larynx. For the defence, Smith stated that he had been unable to find the bruise. Spilsbury then shakily retorted that it had been there when he had conducted his initial examination, but it had since disappeared. Nevertheless, Spilsbury was held in such high regard (earlier in his career, his evidence had helped to convict Dr Hawley Crippen for the murder of his wife) that the jury chose to believe him, rather than Smith, and Fox was duly convicted of murder. Smith died in 1969, and to the end he remained convinced that Mrs Fox had been killed by shock rather than strangulation.

Along with Simpson, Smith helped to push forensic science forward in the 1950s and 1960s (Spilsbury died in 1947). Even so, by the 1960s, a police force investigating a murder could call upon relatively few scientific techniques and forensic experts. Largely they still relied on fingerprints, witnesses and informants. However, we should give credit to Glasgow CID and especially Joe Beattie for commissioning portraits of the man seen with Mima and Helen, as well as a plaster cast of his distinctive teeth. It will be remembered that officers involved in the Bible John inquiry also spoke with tailors, dentists, golf club secretaries and barbers, and made contact with the army, navy and RAF.

Two more experts contributed to that inquiry. The first did work that remains of interest and deserves greater scrutiny. The second, by all accounts, was a fraud.

Profile of a Sadistic Killer

In the late 1960s Dr Robert Brittain – Consultant Forensic Psychiatrist at the Douglas Inch Clinic in Glasgow prior to his death in 1971 – was probably Scotland's most distinguished forensic psychiatrist. He had initially taught in American universities and practised in prisons, and on his return to Britain he took up an appointment as Senior Registrar in Psychiatry at Broadmoor Hospital. In 1963 he moved to Carstairs State Mental Hospital in Scotland, and from 1964 to 1968 he was the Physician Superintendent at Carstairs, prior to moving to the Douglas Inch Clinic. Carstairs opened in 1936 to house people who at that time were described as 'mental defectives'. To this day, it remains one of just four high-security hospitals in the United Kingdom, accommodating mentally disordered, dangerous and violent patients from Scotland and Northern Ireland. Unsurprisingly, given his background (one of Dr Brittain's areas of research was into sadistic, psychopathic killers), Glasgow CID asked him if he would offer an opinion about the type of person Bible John might be. In other words – long before the term was coined – the police were asking for a profile of the killer. What Dr Brittain went on to produce can be compared with our profile of Bible John (see Chapter 4).

It should be noted that Dr Brittain agreed to help Glasgow

CID several years before the FBI started to take an interest in serial killers, so he would not have known about their classification of offenders as either 'organised' or 'disorganised'. Indeed, it could be claimed that the paper he subsequently wrote – 'The Sadistic Murderer' – was the world's first criminal profile. In its introduction, Dr Brittain explains that his work on the Bible John case drew on 'Over twenty years of experience in forensic pathology and forensic psychiatry, from observing scenes of crime, from the examination of the victims and, above all, from the examination and continued study of sexual murderers themselves rather than from psychiatric theory.' The FBI's profilers generally draw on similar experience.

Dr Brittain suggested to detectives looking for Bible John that the man they were seeking was probably under thirty-five years of age, introverted and withdrawn, with few close associates or friends. His interests were therefore solitary; for example, he would not be interested in team sports. He would be well mannered – to the point of being described as 'prim and proper' – but uncommunicative. Anyone who did manage to get to know him would view him as obsessive. He would have a rich fantasy life, often imagining sadistic scenes of torture, and this fantasy life would be very important to him. He would be vain, egocentric and excited by weapons. When he killed, he would do so in a frenzy, having planned his attack very carefully, and would feel superior and 'God-like'. Afterwards, he would have no conscience about what he had done. Rather, he would feel relief and satisfaction.

Dr Brittain also said that a serial murderer typically has

a strong, ambivalent relationship to his mother, both loving and hating her. He is often known as a particularly devoted son, emotionally very closely bound to her, bringing her gifts to a degree beyond the ordinary. He is a 'mother's boy' even when adult. There is also a deep hatred of her, not superficially obvious and not always acknowledged even to himself . . . in some cases the father is known to have been very authoritarian and punitive and may have, or have had, employment in civilian life or an appointment in the services consonant with this.

While all of this might be criticised for being merely a list of vague behavioural characteristics, it was based on practical work that Dr Brittain had undertaken with a number of sadistic murderers. Consequently, it was taken very seriously by the police. In his autobiography, Joe Jackson describes how he and the other detectives on the case first met Dr Brittain: 'this guy just arrived. There was no fanfare of trumpets. He simply turned up where we were working, and started to talk to us.' (As we shall see, this lack of 'fanfare' bears favourable comparison with how other 'experts' were brought into the inquiry.) Brittain was 'small, and bent over – he looked like he was sheltering himself from an attack by one of his patients'. But while Jackson was underwhelmed by the psychiatrist's physique, he was very impressed by his work, especially as Brittain's ideas were presented to the police in a down-to-earth manner. Jackson, for one, thought that he showed great insight and authority.

Unfortunately, though, Dr Brittain's work could not be allied to the forensic techniques that routinely assist murder investigations today – simply because they had not yet been developed. Chief among these is DNA profiling, which would not even be trialled until the late 1970s. Nowadays, of course, it often provides the key piece of evidence at a murder trial.

With such genuinely invaluable techniques still far in the future, perhaps it is understandable that desperate detectives who were getting nowhere in the Bible John inquiry turned to more controversial methods, such as clairvoyance.

The Dutchman with the X-Ray Mind

Gerard Croiset has been variously called the 'Radar Brain', the 'Wizard of Utrecht', the 'Man who Mystifies Europe' and the 'Dutchman with the X-Ray Mind'. Admittedly, though, these epithets were largely coined in the 1950s and 1960s, and then popularised by a very sympathetic biography entitled *Croiset the Clairvoyant*, published in 1964. Croiset's reputation has somewhat diminished more recently, and he is now much more likely to be described simply as a fake. He first came to the notice of Professor W. H. C. Tenhaeff of the Parapsychology Institute at the University of Utrecht in 1945, and over time Tenhaeff promoted and proselytised Croiset, whom he dubbed a 'paragnost'. This is a conflation of two Greek words – *para*, 'beyond'; and *gnosis*, 'knowledge'. However, Croiset was essentially a clairvoyant who specialised in missing persons cases, particularly those involving children. If he was given an 'inductor' – such as a photograph of the child or a piece of their clothing – he claimed to be able to 'see' the movements of the child and so work out where they were located. Croiset did not even have to visit the sites from where these children disappeared – he would often construct a picture from letters and maps of the area and then relay his results over the telephone. His credulous biographer – Jack Harrison Pollack – provides a number of examples of Croiset's successes and is moved to observe: 'If I had not eye-witnessed some of this Dutch sensitive's fantastic feats, I probably would have remained a disbeliever just as are many who did not see firsthand the miracles of the Bible.' In short, Pollack was a true believer.

One 'fantastic feat' provided by Pollack related to a missing four-year-old girl in New York in February 1961. Edith Kiecorius lived in Brooklyn and had been missing for four days when Croiset was consulted. The Dutch airline KLM offered to fly him to New York – no doubt hoping for some reflected publicity – but Croiset said that he could locate Edith simply by being given a photograph of the girl and a map of New York. Pollack writes that Croiset was almost immediately able to confirm that the child was dead and then described where her body might be found:

If you were standing with your back to the Statue of Liberty, it ought to be on the left hand side of New York. There, the child must be! I see a tall building, but that does not mean a thing. There are many tall buildings in New York. But on top of this building, I see an orange rectangular advertisement sign and garage ... rolling shutters ... a square ... and a park ... I see a railway nearby and rails above the street level. Beyond it some rubbish ... and after that some water. There is a river quite near. The man who took the child is small, about fifty-four or fifty-five years of age. He has a rather sharp face . . . he wears something in grey . . . His origin is south European . . . I see a grey house . . . that is where the child is or has been.

Edith – who had been raped – was eventually found dead, and Fred J. Thompson was convicted of her murder. But Thompson – who was later declared insane – was from England, rather than southern Europe, and it is difficult to match Croiset's description of where the little girl would be found with where her body was finally located. Even Pollack had to admit that 'exactly how helpful Croiset was to the New York police in this case may never be known'.

Croiset became involved in the Bible John case in 1970 when the *Daily Record*'s crime correspondent Arnot McWhinnie invited him to Scotland. Initially, Croiset was consulted about the disappearance of a Dumfries teenager, Pat McAdam, but when Joe Beattie heard that the clairvoyant was in the country, discreet enquiries were made to see if he would offer an opinion about Bible John. At the *Daily Record* offices, Croiset drew pictures of where he thought the murderer could be found, which he further suggested was in the south-west of Glasgow, in the general direction of Govan. McWhinnie passed all of these details on to the police, while the paper ran the story for the next two days. Beattie even issued a press statement indicating that they were taking Croiset's views very seriously. However, extensive door-to-door enquiries in and around Govan proved fruitless. As one detective working on the case has since put it, 'the information he provided, regarding a street in Govan, revealed very little'.

This was not the first time that Croiset had spectacularly

failed. On Australia Day in January 1966, three young children had gone missing from Glenelg Beach, near Adelaide. Nine-year-old Jane Beaumont, her seven-year-old sister Arnna and their four-year-old brother Grant had all been seen playing with a tall, blond man, but then they disappeared. A follower of Croiset sent him photographs of the beachfront and some press cuttings, and Croiset suggested a number of places where the children might be found. His Australian supporters dug in sandhills, in a blocked storm drain and in the yard of a school. However, Jane, Arnna and Grant remained missing, so Croiset himself travelled to Adelaide in 1967. At a press conference at the airport, he claimed that he would be able to locate the children. Over the course of the next few days, he suggested one location after another where he thought the children might be discovered – including under the floor of a newly built warehouse, which eventually had to be replaced at a cost of $7,000 – but there was still no trace of them. Nevertheless, his followers retained their faith. Indeed, as recently as 1996, sixteen years after Croiset's death, some of them re-excavated the warehouse. They did not find the Beaumont children.

However, even today, clairvoyance is still occasionally used by police forces and those in search of lost loved ones. In 2007, Portuguese police followed up hundreds of reports from psychics and clairvoyants who claimed to know the whereabouts of Madeleine McCann, who had disappeared from the holiday resort of Praia da Luz in May that year. The Policia Judiciara eventually amassed two eight-centimetre-thick dossiers of apparent visions and sightings of Madeleine at locations all over the world. Several addresses in the UK were raided on the basis of this information. It was also reported that Madeleine's family considered employing a psychic to help locate their daughter.

Glasgow CID's appeal to a psychic indicates similar desperation in their hunt for Bible John. But it would be almost another twenty years before a more legitimate technique was developed to the point where it might assist in uncovering the identity of the murderer.

Colin Pitchfork and DNA

DNA is the genetic material of a cell. Analysis of human tissue or bodily fluids can be used to identify an individual with an incredibly high degree of accuracy. This process, known as 'DNA profiling' or 'DNA fingerprinting', was first used to catch a killer in Britain (or indeed anywhere else in the world) in 1987. At the time, Leicestershire Police were trying to find the murderer of fifteen-year-old Lynda Mann, who had been found raped and strangled in the village of Narborough in 1983, as well as the person responsible for the death of another fifteen-year-old, Dawn Ashworth, who was strangled and sexually assaulted in a village close to Narborough three years later. Having exhausted most of their leads, the police contacted Professor Alec Jeffreys, a geneticist at Leicester University, who had developed a technique (called restriction fragment length polymorphism – RFLP) that could create an individual's genetic fingerprint from a sample of their semen, saliva or blood. Semen had been found on the bodies of Lynda and Dawn, and this was used to build the DNA profile of their killer. The police then asked all the men in the local area between the ages of sixteen and thirty-four to provide blood samples, and from these more DNA profiles were created and compared with that of the killer.

In August 1987, the police received information from a woman working in a local bakery that one of her co-workers, Ian Kelly, had taken the blood test for another employee, Colin Pitchfork. Apparently, Pitchfork had convinced Kelly that he had already given a sample to help out another friend, who had a criminal record, and didn't want to run the risk of being arrested for deception. Before long, he was arrested for much more than that. Pitchfork himself had a criminal record for exposure, and when the police pulled him in for questioning, he readily confessed to the double murder. He was sentenced to life imprisonment in January 1988.

Since Pitchfork's conviction, the science of DNA profiling has advanced greatly, to the point where it is now a standard weapon in the police's armoury. While in 1987 a considerable quantity of cellular material was needed for the RFLP technique to create a profile, today the smallest traces of skin, saliva, blood, hair, sweat or semen are sufficient. These are subjected to allele-specific testing, short tandem repeats' (STRs) and the process of polymerase chain reaction (PCR). The latest technique produces what is called low copy number (LCN) DNA evidence. This has been in development only since 1999, and it allows forensic scientists to build profiles from minute amounts of cellular material. However, it has to be used with considerable care, because very small samples are easily contaminated.

In the Bible John case, semen stains found on Helen Puttock's stocking were used to generate a DNA profile of her killer in the mid-1990s. This, in turn, ruled out John McInnes as a suspect when his body was exhumed in 1996. But Joe Jackson contends that this whole exercise was futile anyway, because of the improper way the samples were stored at the time of the investigation and in the years that followed:

> Physical evidence like stained clothing was very poorly stored and preserved at the time of the inquiry. For instance, bloodstained clothing used to be stored in plastic bags, which caused them to ferment eventually . . . I cannot say for certain how the tights in this case were stored but I cannot see them being treated as gingerly as would be necessary for a clear DNA comparison.

If what Jackson says is correct, and there is every reason to think that it is, a potentially crucial piece of evidence that could have been used to identify Bible John gradually became worthless over the years. It will probably now never generate a DNA profile that will allow any individual, including Peter Tobin, to be linked conclusively with Helen's murder.

While that is frustrating, millions of other samples that are now held in Britain's DNA database have been handled with much more care, and any one of them might eventually provide a crucial piece of evidence in a murder inquiry. Established in 1995, this is the oldest national DNA database in the world, containing samples from some five million people. When it was first established, only those with a criminal record were added to the database, but now anyone who is arrested for an offence that might lead to imprisonment is subjected to a mouth swab, the results of which are then stored. This has already led to some notable convictions, including that of James Lloyd, the 'shoe rapist', who assaulted a number of women between 1983 and 1986 in Rotherham and Barnsley. Lloyd's DNA was not on the database, but after his sister was arrested for drink-driving, hers was added. When the police reopened the shoe rapist case, this 'familial DNA' linked Lloyd to semen samples taken from the women who had been attacked.

Forensic Science and the National DNA Database in Action – Steve Wright

The murders of five young women who worked in the sex industry in Ipswich in late 2006 made national and international news. The pressure on the local police to catch the perpetrator was intense, and one of the key decisions made by the Suffolk Police was to call in the services of the Forensic Science Service (FSS) – an executive agency of the Home Office – at an early stage of their investigation. It is commonly believed that the FSS deals only with offender profiling, but in fact it has a variety of experts at its disposal, and many of these were employed in the Ipswich investigation. The experts work on the basis of there being an 'interchange' between the offender and the victim. They might include those with backgrounds in blood spatter patterns, DNA, firearms, clothing, fibres, hair and bite marks. In a phrase made famous by Edward Locard, they conduct their work under the assumption that 'every contact leaves a trace'. Suffolk Police also utilised a series of national databases, including the Homicide Index (HI), CATCHEM (Centralised Analytical Team Collating Homicide Expertise and Management), CCA (Comparative Case Analysis), BADMAN (Behavioural

Analysis Data Management Auto-indexing Network) and SCAS (Serious Crime Analysis Section).

It might often seem like forensic science is now infallible, having become almost synonymous with certainty, self-discipline, objectivity, truth and justice – not to mention, following the popularity of the American TV series *CSI*, glamour. Ever more frequently we hear news of an offender like James Lloyd being caught by a DNA profiling technique that has allowed a cold case finally to be solved. Even so, on the very day that Lloyd was convicted in 2006, a juror from the trial of Barry George – who was given a life sentence in 2001 for the murder of Jill Dando – broke her silence to say that she felt she had been 'tricked' into convicting George. A number of scientists quickly lent their support to the juror by saying that forensic evidence relating to gunpowder residue supposedly found on George's overcoat was suspect and should have been dismissed as 'unreliable'. Soon a retrial was ordered, and George was finally acquitted in 2008.

Other cases cast doubt on forensic scientists' reputation for meticulous, even obsessive, attention to detail. The scientists who examined the bloodstained shoes of Damilola Taylor failed to notice that some of the spots of blood belonged to the killers rather than the victim. The truth came to light only after the shoes were re-examined by a private forensic science company. Partly as a result of that company's findings, two brothers were eventually convicted of Damilola's manslaughter.

Such mistakes and oversights should perhaps lead us to question what forensic science is, and to look into its limitations when it is applied within the criminal justice and legal systems. The key word here is 'science', which after years of seemingly irresistible academic and popular ascendancy has recently lost some of its cachet. The so-called principles under which it operates suddenly seem less rigorous than the scientists have led us to believe, with conjecture, prejudice and error much more prevalent in the scientific community than was previously thought. So the time seems right to reassess what forensic science can – and what it cannot – achieve.

For instance, in the Steve Wright case, there were some problems that no amount of forensic science could overcome. The police's *Murder Investigation Manual* identifies five possible significant sites that require forensic analysis:

- Last seen alive site
- Initial contact site
- 'Attack' site
- Murder site
- Body dump site

In Ipswich, the police were unable to establish the attack site, the murder site or the initial contact site for any of Wright's murders. Partly that was why so much energy was expended on more traditional methods of enquiry, such as trying to establish the final movements of the five victims. It also explains why the body dump sites became so crucial. Even so, forensic analysis of these sites was only ever going to get the police so far – in spite of the inflated claims of some of the scientists themselves.

Fortunately, Wright's DNA was on the national database as a result of his being convicted of stealing £80 from his employer five years earlier. He could not have known then just how important that theft would become, because it would help to convict him of murder. However, once the police had found their prime suspect through the database, they had to build a case against him. That included methodically studying his mobile phone records and taking detailed statements from witnesses who had seen his car in Ipswich's red-light district. In short, DNA analysis and profiling is now a very useful weapon in the fight against serious crime, but it is not the be all and end all. The police still need to do the basics well, too.

Chapter Eight

A Bridge from the Present to the Past

This is it, I have found the man of my dreams.

Margaret Mackintosh

Beneath the exterior of self-serving charm and urbanity – which most psychopaths can usually switch on or off at will – the crocodile smile, which doesn't quite vitalise the eyes, there exist only negative emotions, all of which are primarily concerned with personal ambition and the will to power.

Ian Brady, *The Gates of Janus: Serial Killing and Its Analysis*

For Peter Tobin, being married was simply a means of controlling another person, dictating her actions and, as he saw it, 'owning' the ability to have sex whenever he wanted. Love, or the apparent process of falling in love, was quickly replaced

with violence and rape. Another way to describe Tobin's relationships is that he was 'angry, unpredictable, demanding and
dominating' – a phrase we used in our profile of Bible John. As
we build our bridge from the present to the past, other Bible
John characteristics also chime with Tobin's history, including
both men's links with Glasgow.

Margaret Mackintosh told us that she was 'brought up prim
and proper'. So when she met a young man who was kind,
handsome, well dressed and a 'gentleman' – he would open
the door of his car for her before whisking her off to Loch
Lomond, then bring her back to her home in Earlbank
Avenue, Scotstoun, promptly at 10.30 p.m., as her parents had
demanded – Margaret thought he was the 'man of my dreams'.
His name was Peter Tobin. She was only seventeen when she
first met the twenty-year-old Tobin at the dancing at the
Highland Institute in Glasgow in August 1968; and while her
parents weren't as impressed by her new man as she was,
Margaret was more than happy. In fact, she was infatuated,
describing herself as 'emphatically in love'. She even went to
see his parents – although only once. She remembered that
they were an elderly couple who 'stared out into space', and
that their house in Paisley, south of the river, was dark and
filled with crucifixes and rosary beads. Margaret was a
Protestant, while Tobin was a quite religious Catholic who
clearly knew a lot about his faith. However, he never went so
far as to quote from the Bible. Later, having lost contact with
Margaret, her distraught mother first tracked down Tobin's
parents, then went to see the family's priest. 'Oh dear,' said the
priest, 'she's not found a good one there.'

Pretty soon after their first meeting, Tobin asked Margaret

to visit him in his flat in Shettleston. She could not understand how he managed to afford the place, nor even where he found the money to run a car, as he never mentioned doing any type of work. Margaret vividly remembers her first visit to the flat:

> He was still the nice guy – loving, tender, plenty of good physical lovemaking. We laughed, we chatted, we were just happy. He asked if I would like to stay the night. I said, 'No.' He said, 'I think that you should stay the night.' I got up and went towards the door, but he pulled me back. It was like being kidnapped for a year. I didn't have any clean clothes.

Margaret was effectively imprisoned in the flat in Shettleston and then in another in Brighton before she managed to return home. The physical and mental scars of those twelve months endure to this day. We interviewed her at length because we wanted to learn what it was like to be 'married' to Peter Tobin, in Glasgow, at the moment when the Bible John murders began.

Peter Tobin in the Late 1960s

Margaret was often raped, up to three times a day. The handsome, polite and charming man with whom she had been 'emphatically in love' turned into a monster, and their relationship mutated from being 'normal' to one in which she was threatened almost constantly. Tobin, for example, told Margaret he would stab her if she ever stepped out of line. Their sex life was violent, 'always rough', in Margaret's words. She also recalls: 'When I was menstruating, it didn't stop him.

He seemed to get more excited because of the blood. I had no protection – I had to wrap up bits of old paper, and use that as a sanitary towel. His attitude was "So what?" It didn't bother him that my period was sore – he just carried on regardless.' On one occasion, Tobin actually used a knife on Margaret after she complained that she was having her period:

> He said, 'That doesn't matter,' and carried on. I was crying and I had had enough, but we had a bed in an alcove and he pulled me up onto that. I was crying and he kept telling me to shut up, and he couldn't perform well with one hand over my mouth. Once he was finished he just said, 'This will stop you screaming,' and he pulled out his knife and pushed it inside me, turning it like a corkscrew. You could say it was a metal Tampax. I could never have children because of this incident.

Margaret was so badly injured that her blood dripped from the bed to the floor and then started to seep through the ceiling of the flat below. The downstairs neighbour eventually called an ambulance, which took Margaret to Glasgow's Western Infirmary. His prompt action probably saved her life. Even so, there was to be no relief. The first person Margaret saw when she woke up in her hospital bed was Tobin: 'He didn't ask how I was – he just said, "Hello." I don't know why the doctors didn't question him more closely, but he seems to have come up with some excuse about having been away on business, that we had been burgled, and that this was what the burglar had done to me.'

Margaret didn't go to the police, or make contact with her

parents, or even ask the medical staff to make contact with them on her behalf, simply because she was too scared of the consequences if she did. Some understanding of her emotions can be gleaned from the fact that she describes herself as having been 'kidnapped'. Psychologists are now very familiar with 'Stockholm syndrome – a psychological condition first identified in the aftermath of an attempted robbery of the Kreditbanken in Stockholm on 23 August 1973. A number of bank employees were held hostage for five days, and during their captivity they formed emotional bonds with the machine-gun-carrying robber and his accomplice. This in spite of the fact that, at one stage, nooses were put around their necks and the robbers threatened to shoot them if their demands were not met. The hostages may have come to believe that the robbers were actually protecting them from the police, and even after the siege ended they refused to give evidence against their captors. The term 'Stockholm syndrome' was coined by the Swedish psychiatrist who advised the police during the robbery – Nils Bejerot – but it is now used more generally to describe the 'love' that an abused person can feel for their abuser. In short, if the former cannot escape from the latter, if they are kept in isolation and are regularly threatened, they gradually take the side of the abuser, or at least don't go out of their way to cause any trouble.

From more recent times, we can see another example of Stockholm syndrome in the behaviour of fourteen-year-old Elizabeth Smart, who was kidnapped from her home in Salt Lake City, Utah, on 5 June 2002. Brian David Mitchell and his wife Wanda Eileen Barzee allegedly held Elizabeth captive for nine and a half months. (Mitchell has never been convicted of the crime because he has been deemed 'mentally incompetent' to stand trial, while Barzee was recently sentenced to fifteen years' imprisonment for her lesser role in the kidnapping.) However, it seems that minimum force (or none whatsoever) was needed to keep Elizabeth captive: she was moved frequently from one location to another yet never cried out for help; and she initially did not want to give the police her true identity, having been found wearing a wig, sunglasses and a veil. This apparent loyalty to her captors developed even though Elizabeth was allegedly shackled, threatened and raped repeatedly, having been told that it was God's will for her to become Mitchell's second wife.

Stockholm syndrome provides a useful context within which to view and examine Margaret's predicament and her reaction to it. She was unable to make contact with her parents at a time before mobile phones and the internet, and she was regularly threatened by Tobin, who often reminded her that he carried a knife and proved that he was willing to use it. The only clothes she had for the whole year were those she had worn when she first arrived at the flat, and she was dependent upon Tobin for food. Whenever they left the flat together (which was rare – she was usually kept locked up for days on end), Tobin always walked on the outside of the pavement. This ties in with his view of himself as a gentleman, as the practice had first developed to protect a lady from passing horses, carts and, later, cars. However, in this case, it was probably more intended to stop Margaret from running across the road, where she might have been able to find assistance. Later, when they lived in Brighton, if a police car passed along the street, Tobin would push Margaret into the nearest shop so she couldn't be seen.

Nevertheless, Margaret was allowed to cultivate a friendship with a woman who lived in the flat beside Tobin's in Shettleston. She would sometimes even babysit the woman's children. By this stage, Tobin must have felt that he could trust Margaret sufficiently to 'normalise' their lives, to some extent at least. He even agreed to Margaret's request for a puppy to keep her company when Tobin disappeared during the day. In due course he brought home a beautiful, black Labrador, just six to eight weeks old. Margaret named the puppy Bute, and remembers that he liked to play between her feet and fall asleep on her lap. However, he also 'yapped a lot and peed and messed on the floor, and I was the one to clean up after him'. One day, Margaret left the flat to talk to Tobin's neighbour, and there was no sign of the dog when she returned:

I looked everywhere for Bute. I looked out of the top window down to where kids were kicking an object around, like a football. I rang the bell next door and asked the boys if they had seen Bute. 'Yes,' they said, 'he's in the backyard'. I rushed down the landing and into the yard, but Bute was nowhere to be seen. There were other boys playing there, so I asked them if they had seen a black puppy. 'Yes,' one said, and pointed behind me. 'There's its body and here's its head,' he continued, kicking a black object towards me. It was Bute's head. I don't know how I managed to run back upstairs – I was physically sick and shaking. I sat on the edge of the bed crying and screaming.

I was just on my way back next door when Tobin arrived. He pushed me back inside and hauled me by the arm into the living room. 'Stop screaming! Stop yelling!' he ordered. 'I was fed up of the dog's yelping and mess so I chopped off its head and threw it out of the window.' He was smiling.

This incident – which preceded Tobin's knife attack on Margaret herself – is full of details that need to be carefully analysed. Specifically, the sadism displayed by Tobin is worthy of comment. Sadism – unlike brutality – often feeds off empathy. In other words, such behaviour is ingrained and perpetual, and it demands a reaction from the person who is the object of the sadism. Sadists need their victim to cry, scream, show fear or pain, as this reaction sustains and then encourages similar behaviour in the future. By contrast, a brutal act might occur on the spur of the moment, in response to specific circumstances, and the person committing the act does not require the object of his brutality to react. As such, it might be a one-off.

Margaret started to grow fond of the puppy, which had two consequences. First, her attention was drawn away from Tobin's needs and desires, which he would have found intolerable, given that sadists always need to be the centre of attention. Second, by killing the much-loved puppy, Tobin was able to demonstrate his complete control over everything that came into (or, indeed, left) the flat. Bute's death was a stark reminder to Margaret of Tobin's capacity for violence, which was why he did not want to hide what he had done to the puppy. He could have buried the dog, then claimed that it had run away or been knocked down by a car, but that would not have served his purpose. He wanted Margaret to know that he was responsible for chopping off Bute's head and throwing it out of the window. The very public violation of the dog's head and body by the group of boys was exactly the gruesome turn of events he hoped to achieve. He wanted Margaret to know that he was capable of such extreme cruelty, and he wanted to witness her reaction to gaining that knowledge. Of course, his excuse for his behaviour – that the dog yelped and made a mess – was little more than a fig leaf to hide the contempt, control and mastery that he wished to exercise over Margaret. In the end, he achieved his goal, as Margaret herself admits. She describes herself as being 'disarrayed, disorientated, faint, a puppet' during the twelve months she lived with Peter Tobin.

The Banality of Evil

Margaret is able to provide other glimpses of her year with Tobin. We have chosen the word 'glimpses' very carefully, to indicate that the view she provides is brief, incomplete and vague. We certainly believe what Margaret has to say, but she no longer remembers every detail perfectly, and she can be unclear about times, locations and even quite mundane facts about Tobin. After all, it must be remembered that Tobin had complete control over Margaret's life, so she knew not to ask certain questions that would be considered routine within a normal relationship. If she did ever ask such questions, Tobin would have felt no obligation to answer. For example, we asked Margaret what job Tobin did when they were together, but she didn't know. All she said was: 'He never told me

Police uncover the remains of two bodies in Tobin's back garden. These are later confirmed to be Vicky Hamilton and Dinah McNicol. *Sky News*

Police found this knife stashed in Tobin's loft. Traces of Vicky Hamilton's DNA were found on the blade. *Sky News*

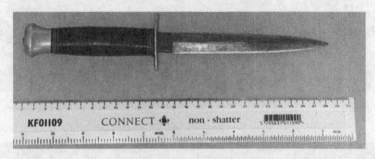

Tobin's knife in police evidence. *Sky News*

Vicky Hamilton's purse was a key piece of evidence in convicting Tobin. Tobin had disposed of the purse in Edinburgh, where it had been handed into the police and returned to her family. Sixteen years later police discovered traces of Tobin's son's DNA on the purse – he had been allowed to play with it before his father threw it away. *Sky News*

Tobin being interviewed by the police. He denied ever having met Vicky Hamilton. *Sky News*

Peter Tobin is lead into court in handcuffs during the Dinah McNicol trial. *PA Photos/Topfoto*

Tobin lashes out at a photographer on his way into court. *Sky News*

Peter Tobin. *PA Photos/Topfoto*

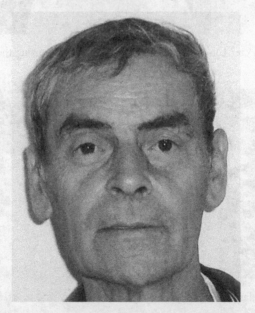

Cathy Wilson, Tobin's third wife and the mother of his son, on her way into court to give evidence.
Sky News

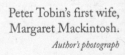

Peter Tobin's first wife, Margaret Mackintosh.
Author's photograph

OPERATION ANAGRAM

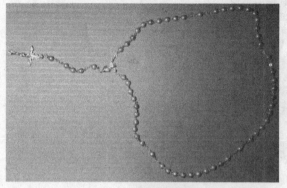

Rosary beads found in Tobin's belongings by Operation Anagram. Police suspect these could be 'trophies', taken from other victims.

Rex Features

Badge of the Royal Electrical and Mechanical Engineers, as found in Tobin's possessions. Helen Puttock's husband served in this regiment.

Rex Features

Religious medals found in Tobin's belongings.

Rex Features

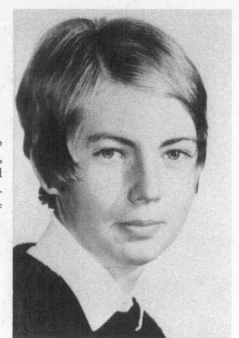

Thirteen-year-old April Fabb disappeared in Norfolk in 1969, between Bible John's second and third known murders. *PA Photos/Topfoto*

Barbara Mayo vanished while hitch-hiking on the M1 in 1970. Her body was found six days later. *PA Photos/Topfoto*

Genette Tate, 13, disappeared in 1978.
Her body has never been found. *Sky News*

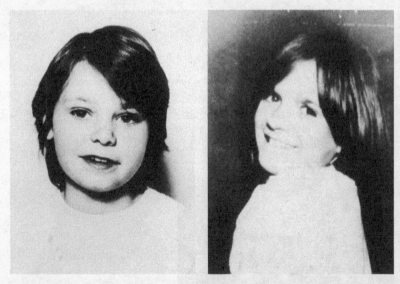

The 'Babes in the Wood', Karen Hadaway, 10, and Nicola Fellows, 9. The girls
were killed in 1986 whilst playing together in Wild Park, Brighton. *Topfoto*

where he was going. He'd literally walk out of the door, and that was that.' However, she suspects that he was a thief, and pawned the items he stole to pay for his car and petrol. Tobin also bought all the food for the two of them, although Margaret is at pains to point out, 'I mean [he bought] milk, bread, coffee, tins of lager. Nothing that could make an actual meal.' Of course, keeping Margaret hungry was another way to maintain control over her. In short, Tobin starved her of both knowledge and food, so any information or morsel seemed like a luxury that had to be savoured and for which she should be grateful. Indeed, that is precisely why Margaret remembers so many details about Bute. She recalls every aspect of the dog's short life and death because they were among the few pieces of information that she, rather than Tobin, controlled at the time.

She also remembers that there was little in the way of decoration or furniture in the flat. As she bleakly puts it, 'We had nothing.' When this is considered alongside the lack of food, clothes and even information about what Tobin was up to, the picture that emerges is one of absence. 'We had nothing' suggests not only the absence of meals to eat and chairs to sit on, but the absence of a real relationship that would nurture and sustain both partners. It was almost as if Tobin created a black hole that sucked everything that was capable of showing – or being shown – love out of the flat. The man who had once charmed and delighted Margaret was only surface deep, so as soon as she was able to look beneath that façade a very different character emerged. She saw a man who was 'cool under pressure. I think that he was totally fearless of everybody and everything. He never seemed scared.'

Margaret believes that Tobin had a good knowledge of the roads in and around Glasgow, largely based on the trips that they took soon after they met. Tobin drove her to Loch Lomond and the Kirkhouse Inn at Strathblane, among other places. Cars always featured prominently in his life, and driving was important for him. It was another way in which he felt in control; it gave him a sense of power. And, as we have seen, it allowed him to meet potential victims and later to dispose of their bodies. Cars, driving and commuting were all central to Tobin's life as a killer.

Margaret clearly remembers some physical details about Tobin from the time when she knew him. He had short brown or dark brown hair, cut away from his face – definitely not a 'Beatles cut'. He was handsome, despite a scar down the side of his left eye, which he told her he got in a fight during his school days. And he would always wear a suit and tie: 'Jeans were in, but he'd never wear them.' He admitted that he'd been in Borstal, although never told Margaret what crime he'd committed. He smoked untipped cigarettes and he was definitely under six feet tall.

Escape from Brighton and Tobin

At the time, Tobin seems to have had only one friend. It appears that this friend suggested to Tobin that he should take Margaret to Brighton. However, details about Tobin's relationship with this man are difficult to establish, and Margaret is far from certain that Tobin was even in contact with him while they lived in Shettleston. Unfortunately, we have been unable to contact this friend to clarify the matter. Nevertheless, we do know that Tobin and Margaret took the bus south – with that part of the trip apparently financed by Tobin stealing and then pawning one of Margaret's aunt's rings – and then hitch-hiked the rest of the way. They broke up the journey with a visit to Margaret's cousin in Acocks Green, Birmingham, but Tobin fought with their host and they soon left.

Once in Brighton they lived near St Michael's Place, where life continued in much the same way as it had in Glasgow. Margaret says she survived on toast and coffee, and still had no new clothes. When Tobin went out during the day – and this time it appears he found himself some form of employment – Margaret was locked in the main room of the flat: 'At least there was a sink in there, as I could not get to the toilet . . . I suppose I would often just sit and cry. Sometimes I was even glad when he came back – it was company and just maybe some decent food.'

It was in Brighton that Margaret finally married Tobin – almost a year to the day after they first met. One day, Tobin insisted that Margaret must sign her father's name, and pushed a pen into her hand. (She was still under eighteen, so needed her parent's permission to marry.) Before long, 'The dreaded day came. He bought me a suit which I was to wear and, from somewhere, he produced a wedding ring. We were married in the Registry Office in Brighton on 6 August 1969.'

The marriage (which, of course, was illegal because the parental permission had been forged) did not change the way that Tobin treated Margaret – he continued to punch, kick and threaten her. Margaret knew she had to escape, and her chance finally came as a result of the police visiting their flat after a complaint had been made against Tobin. Margaret was made to answer the door to the police and tell them Tobin was out. Their visit prompted Tobin to make the decision to leave Brighton, with Margaret, and move to London. With no money for the train fare, they would have to hitch-hike again, so once the coast was clear they set off:

> We started walking on this rather wide pavement towards the motorway – Tobin was again on the outside. The fact that no one was allowed to walk on the motorway didn't seem to deter him. I was trying to think of a way to get help before we got to the motorway, and I saw that there was a café up ahead. I convinced Tobin that we should go in for a coffee, and then said that I needed the toilet. I walked to where the toilet was, then asked a waitress to call the police. She looked at me with a worried and bemused face. 'Please,' I said, 'I'm not joking.'

Now the waitress could see that Margaret was genuine and she did indeed phone the police. However, Tobin realised something was going on and quickly left the café, pulling Margaret down a side road.

> God knows what would have happened to me if I hadn't had the presence of mind, even as an eighteen-year-old, to get the waitress to call the police. The police caught us quickly and we were both arrested. They put us in cells at Brighton police station. The next day we were taken in handcuffs aboard a train back up to Scotland, to Partick police station. A policewoman was with me and he was accompanied by a policeman. When we arrived we were

again placed in cells. The police later called my mother, who came to collect me and took me home. We were both charged with the theft of various things from lots of places and I got a two years' probation.

Tobin also received a suspended sentence, in November 1969, whereupon he returned to the south coast alone. His arrest gave Margaret the opportunity to escape from the evil clutches of her illegitimate husband for good, and she returned to her family in Glasgow. Within eighteen months, he was back inside, serving a seventeen-month sentence at HMP Lewes for burglary. She was sure she would never see him again. But towards the end of the 1970s, while on a train en route to work, she found herself standing opposite Tobin. Petrified that he might recognise her, she got off the train at the first opportunity. She stepped onto an almost deserted platform, where she stood for a moment, praying that Tobin had not followed her. The train pulled away.

It would be almost thirty years before she saw his face again – on TV. Her ex-husband had just been arrested for the murder of Angelika Kluk.

A House Divided

On 6 May 1966, Ian Brady and Myra Hindley were sentenced to life imprisonment. Only the abolition of the death penalty – a month after their arrest – saved them from being hanged. Both are now so associated with the 'Moors murders' that few people realise Brady (who was born Ian Duncan Stewart on 2 January 1938) was brought up in Glasgow, initially in the

Gorbals. But his father had died three months before Brady was born, and his mother was unable to cope on her own, so she arranged to have him looked after by Mary and John Sloan, who lived in Pollock. At the age of eleven, Brady passed a grammar school entrance exam and was enrolled in Shawlands Academy, in the south of the city. The Sloans remembered that he loved trips to Loch Lomond because he had a 'deep affinity with the wild, rugged and empty scenery around the lake. He was moved by the grandeur of the hills, awed by the vastness of the sky.' Although he was intelligent, Brady was a loner, and by the age of thirteen he had already appeared before a juvenile court for burglary. By sixteen, he was working as a tea boy in a Glasgow shipyard, but he was soon in court again. This time it was decided to send him to Manchester, so he could rejoin his mother, who was working there and had married a meat porter by the name of Patrick Brady. Ian Stewart took his stepfather's name, and in less than a decade he would commit the first Moors murder.

Can anything from Brady's history provide an insight into the behaviour of Peter Tobin? Obviously, both had links with the south of Glasgow, but there is also a chilling echo of Brady's love for the wild and rugged scenery around Loch Lomond in Tobin's drives to the loch with Margaret. More-over, both were in trouble with the law at an early age (with Tobin being sent to Borstal), and both travelled to England shortly thereafter. Indeed, both young men possessed a rest-less energy. All of these connections are interesting, but they get us only so far. For a deeper insight, we need to analyse the two men's psychological journeys, and part of the means for doing that comes from Brady himself. While in prison, he wrote a part-autobiography, part-thesis called *The Gates of Janus*.

In the book, Brady quotes extensively from interviews he conducted with a number of fellow serial killers, most notably the Yorkshire Ripper – Peter Sutcliffe. When analysing what these men have to say, Brady makes a particularly telling observation, which was quoted in part at the beginning of this chapter. In full, the passage reads:

Beneath the exterior of self-serving charm and urbanity – which most psychopaths can usually switch on and off at will – the crocodile smile, which doesn't quite vitalise the eyes, there exists only negative emotions, all of which are primarily concerned with personal ambition and the will to power. The most salient traits and characteristics are cold-ness, calculation, manipulation, lack of sensitivity, natural deviousness, facile mendacity, amorality presented as moral flexibility, pathological anger and envy rationalised as altruism or logic, all-encompassing greed, assumption of personal superiority over others, a dictatorial and bullying attitude relying on power and authority rather than intel-ligence, suspicion and lack of trust to a paranoid degree, inexorable ruthlessness, an egocentric conviction that they are always right, sexual promiscuousness, complete lack of remorse.

Here Brady presents his analysis as if he were an objective psychologist dispassionately assessing his patients; but, of course, he is also revealing plenty about *his own* behaviour and what drove *him* to kill. In short, he is describing his own

188 THE LOST BRITISH SERIAL KILLER

'self-serving charm and urbanity' as much as he is describing that of others. It is doubtful that he did this unwittingly (after all, we know that Brady is far from stupid), so we should probably question his motives. However, leaving that aside, to what extent does Brady's description of the 'typical' serial killer help us to understand Tobin, as he was described by Margaret?

At the most obvious level, Margaret thought Tobin was the 'man of my dreams' and a 'gentleman' when they first met. Could there be a better example of the 'self-serving charm and urbanity' that Brady describes? Tobin's charm was manufactured to persuade Margaret first into a relationship and then into his flat in Shettleston. In other words, *his* goals and personal ambitions were being prioritised, rather than Margaret's, even though those goals initially seemed to be shared. Sex was very important to Tobin (he was probably promiscuous), with Margaret noting that he was 'loving [and] tender' and that they enjoyed 'plenty of good physical lovemaking', which only later deteriorated into 'rough sex'. This is merely the most immediate of the 'negative emotions' that Brady describes. The paranoia, lack of trust and suspicion that characterised Tobin's behaviour are obvious in his insistence on locking Margaret in the flat and pushing her into doorways whenever a police car passed them in the street. He was even suspicious of their puppy, which diverted attention away from Tobin himself. Margaret also lets us know that Tobin was 'cool under pressure' and 'never seemed scared'.

In all of this we can glimpse the 'inexorable ruthlessness' that Brady describes, as well as the bullying, the despotism, and Tobin's sense (Brady calls it 'egocentric conviction') that he is always right. Ultimately, this would lead Tobin to find it impossible to show any remorse for his crimes – after all, he cannot understand that he has done anything wrong, so he is able to rationalise away his behaviour. This is best seen in his reaction after the attack on Margaret that left her hospitalised and unable to have children: 'He didn't ask how I was – he just said, "Hello."' He has no sense of the damage that he has caused to Margaret. Or else he simply doesn't care. Her pain and suffering mean nothing to him, so he doesn't find it necessary to show remorse. His 'facile mendacity' has already allowed him to concoct a story to tell the doctors – a burglar did this to Margaret. No doubt he once again turned on his charm and urbanity to ensure that his version of events was believed. Was he scared that he might have been arrested? It seems not. And getting away with the assault would merely have buttressed his sense of 'personal superiority'.

Another passage from Brady's autobiography also helps us to understand some of Tobin's behaviour. In the chapter that he devotes to Peter Sutcliffe, Brady notes it is 'paradoxical that, on the one hand, the serial killer often wishes to demonstrate his contempt of society, yet still feels compelled to maintain his good name, as it were . . . [T]he inner knowledge that he is a house divided slowly corrodes the artificial boundary that the killer has tried to build within to separate his two selves, his dual personality.'

Again, this description fits Ian Brady himself just as neatly as it does Peter Sutcliffe, but the notion of the serial killer trying to maintain a reputation within a culture that he actively despises is still useful. In relation to Tobin, it helps to explain the rather deeper emotions that led him to present himself as a 'gentleman', and it provides a context for other information offered by Margaret: for example, 'jeans were in, but he'd never wear them', and his hair was cut short, away from his face. These were attempts to present himself as part of an older, more established culture, rather than a member of the new cultural order, even though that new order was fashionable and had been adopted by most of his peers. He wanted to be accepted within the culture of his parents – described by Margaret as elderly and living in a house filled with crucifixes – not as an active participant in the 'swinging sixties'. It is significant that he first met Margaret in the sober Highland Institute, rather than at the glitzy, raucous Barrowland Ballroom.

Marital Bliss?

After Tobin was released from prison in October 1972, he needed to find someone new to control. He married thirty-year-old nurse Sylvia Jefferies in Brighton in September 1973, a matter of weeks after they met. But she did not accept his proposal because she was in love with him. She married him out of fear.

Sylvia would eventually describe her life with Tobin in a TV interview she gave to *Five News*:

> I have flashbacks where I'm laying next to him on the bed with his arms around my throat. He was pure evil, absolute evil. I can remember one day being by the window on the floor with the curtain around me. I don't know how it happened, but he must have knocked me across the room. He threatened me with his knife at one point, telling me, 'I'm going to kill you.' His temper would just go, and it would go by hitting the wall, hitting the door, hitting me.

But Sylvia would still give birth to Tobin's first son. Unsurprisingly, given that he had recently been driven to fury by his previous wife's affection for a puppy, Tobin found it hard to adapt to having a baby in the house: 'The rocking of the cot would drive him mad, so I used to go to the baby and say, "Please be quiet, please be quiet, or you'll make him cross."' Their second child, Claire, would survive for just two days before dying from breathing difficulties. The tragedy prompted Sylvia to make her getaway: 'I feel that she died so that we could escape from him. It was easier to run away with one child than it would have been with two. And it was like she was saying to me: 'Right, Mum, go!'

As soon as Sylvia returned to the ground-floor flat she shared with Tobin, she began to plan her escape. She found the number of a women's refuge, called them, and was told that they would provide a safe house in London. Then she waited for Tobin to go out. When he finally did, she packed a carrier bag, grabbed the pushchair and put her son inside, fled to the station and got on the first train. She didn't even know where they were heading, but she didn't care. For years after, she feared that Tobin was searching for them. She was probably right to be concerned, but he never found them.

Tobin is thought to have remained predominantly on the south coast during most of the seventies and eighties, even though he had no particular links to the area, save for a small number of friends and acquaintances. He would pick up work where and when he could, and some reports have him running a tea shop and working in a hotel in Eastbourne.

He met his third wife, sixteen-year-old insurance clerk

Cathy Wilson, in October 1986 at a dancehall in Brighton. Cathy fell for the charming older man (Tobin was now forty) and they began to sleep together. Initially, Tobin managed to suppress his violent tendencies, but he was just as devious as ever. To convince her to agree to unprotected sex, he told Cathy he was about to have an operation that would leave him infertile. After conning his young girlfriend into falling pregnant, Tobin quickly swapped charm for physical and psychological abuse. On the day that she went into labour in 1988, he refused to take her to hospital until she had prepared a roast dinner for him and his friends. When she was finally admitted, she gave birth to the one strong tie in Tobin's life – his son Daniel.

Despite Tobin's apparent personality change, the couple subsequently married at a Methodist church in Brighton. Soon thereafter, Tobin insisted on applying for a council house exchange, which was what led to the family moving to Bathgate in October 1989. Cathy later explained: 'He was all sweetness until he had me where he wanted me. Once I was pregnant, he changed, and used Daniel to control me.' Completely isolated from her family and friends, and with no financial independence, Cathy was now entirely at Tobin's mercy, and constantly fearful for the safety of her child. She recalls, 'He was so volatile and kept me in fear. Moving me to Scotland, where I knew no one, felt like the final nail.' The charming man who had swept Cathy of her feet at the dancehall had disappeared, replaced by a violent and controlling bully. 'If he said something and I dared to speak back or answer him in a way he thought disrespectful he would blow up. If I made dinner and he didn't like it, he would throw the plate at me, telling me I was stupid.' She was allowed to call her grandparents once a week, but Tobin would always supervise the calls and 'monitor' what she was saying. She wasn't even allowed into their back garden to play with Daniel without him accompanying her, in case she spoke to a neighbour and revealed what was going on. On one rare occasion when Cathy built up the courage to tell Tobin that she was leaving him, and taking Daniel with her, he responded with a terrifying threat. She describes the horrifying scene: 'He lifted Daniel up, carried him to the top of the stairs and lifted him over his head, challenging me with the most hideous glare. "If you try to leave me, I'll kill him," he said and made as if to throw him.

When Tobin had first seen Cathy at the dancehall in Brighton, she had been a very slim adolescent. Now he took pleasure in bringing home virtually emaciated teenage prostitutes. He would make his wife watch as he stripped the girls and had rough and often painful sex with them. Cathy soon realised that many of the girls resembled her, but it seemed to be their thinness that really excited Tobin. Performing violent sex in front of his wife made him feel powerful. He would place a collar and leash around the prostitutes' necks, which at times nearly choked them, and would tie their hands behind their backs, using Cathy's scarf. If they moaned with pain and tried to resist, that would excite him; but if they complained, he would strike them hard across the face, then remind them that he had paid extra for this type of 'service'. If Cathy bravely tried to intervene to help the girls, that would only get Tobin even more excited. Finally, after each sordid, violent session with a prostitute, Tobin would demand rough sex from his wife, too. Cathy could do no more than let him have his way.

But Tobin was starting to get a bad reputation in the local red-light district as word of his increasing violence spread. Cathy believes the last prostitute to visit the house had been very reluctant to come with Tobin, but she had been desperate for the money so had finally agreed. She left a few hours later, battered and bruised, but at least able to walk out of the front door. Eleven months later, Vicky Hamilton would not be so lucky.

But by then, Cathy was no longer living in Bathgate. Almost two years of marital abuse was as much as she could take. One evening, Tobin decided to go to a car auction, after complaining that his car had become unreliable. Before he left, he made sure to grab Cathy's driving licence, bank book, money and keys, thinking that would prevent her getting very far, should she be foolish enough to try. He told her he would be gone for an hour and a half. She had to act quickly, of course, but she was helped by the fact that she had been planning for this moment for quite some time. She had been collecting ten pence here, fifty pence there, and she now had £25 in her escape fund. It wasn't much, but it would buy her and Daniel a bus ticket away from the man who was making their lives a misery. At the bus station, she shook with fear, convinced that Tobin was already on his way to find them. But they made it to Glasgow, then on to an overnight bus to London and, finally, to the safety of her grandparents' home in Portsmouth.

Tobin had been outwitted again, but he wasn't about to let the matter rest. He arranged the move to Margate to be closer to his son and started demanding frequent access visits. And this latest council house exchange had an added bonus – it allowed Tobin to bury the remains of Vicky Hamilton five hundred miles from where she had disappeared.

Although Cathy was reluctant to allow Tobin access to Daniel, she was terrified of the repercussions of denying him visits with his son. With some caution, she allowed them to spend time together. Then, one weekend, Tobin called Cathy to say that he was taking Daniel back to Scotland and that she would never see her son again. At that point, Cathy realised that she would have to become devious herself. She made Tobin think she was starting to enjoy his company again, and spent ever more time with him. All along, though, she was in the process of obtaining a court order granting her full custody of Daniel.

However, a furious Tobin stayed close by, and eventually he regained the right to see his son. Throughout the latter half of 1991, Daniel visited Tobin's house in Margate, where he played a few feet above the bodies of Vicky Hamilton and Dinah McNicol. Perhaps worried by what his son might dig up, Tobin decided it was time to move on. He rented a flat in Leigh Park, near Havant, which made picking up and dropping off Daniel much easier. Yet again, though, there was an ulterior motive for his latest relocation.

New pastures. New victims.

1993 – The Summer of Sex, Drugs and Teenagers

Tobin answered the door, even though he hadn't been expecting any visitors to his second-floor council flat. Before him stood two fourteen-year-old girls who had come to the block of flats to visit the woman next door, but she was out. Tobin knew one of the girls, and suggested that they could wait until his neighbour returned. It wouldn't be long, he assured them. Daniel was staying with him that August day, but he was playing happily in another room. That meant Tobin could take full advantage of the unexpected opportunity that had just presented itself. As soon as the girls were through the front door, he began plying them with cider and vodka. He also gave them two small tablets, telling them he had taken some himself that day. The girls only pretended to take the pills – dropping them into their pockets when Tobin wasn't looking – but the alcohol soon started to take effect. One of the girls fell over in front of the fire as she got up from the sofa. The other returned from the bathroom, where she had been sick, and tried to wake up her friend, who was now semi-conscious on the living-room floor. It was at that point that Tobin turned violent. He threatened the girl with a bread knife and told her he would kill her if she continued to cry. Then he forced her to take a cocktail of pills and wine. She tried to make a run for it, but Tobin grabbed her around the throat. During the struggle that ensued, she managed to stab him in the leg with the knife. When five-year-old Daniel suddenly appeared in the room, the girl pleaded with him to get help, but he was quickly dispatched from the room by Tobin. It wasn't long before she was unconscious. She was then raped and sodomised by Tobin.

By the time he had finished, the forty-six-year-old was anxious. He knew the families of the two girls would soon wonder why they hadn't returned home, or indeed even turned up at his neighbour's house. For all he knew, a search of the flats might already be under way. It was 2 a.m. Tobin realised he would have to disappear quickly. He phoned Cathy, waking her up, and asked her to come and collect Daniel. The preposterous excuse he gave was that he was having a heart attack and needed to go to hospital. By the time she arrived, Tobin was waiting at the foot of the stairs with their son. He also had a bag of items that Cathy identified as personal belongings which Tobin would have wanted Daniel to have, in case he never saw his son again. Tobin assured Cathy he would be OK, she left with Daniel, and Tobin went back upstairs. He locked all the doors, packed a bag of belongings and turned the gas fire fully on, but did not ignite it. Then he opened a window and slid down the drainpipe.

But his plan to gas the girls failed. Shortly after 6 a.m., one of them awoke to find a bloodied bandage around her wrist, a tie around her ankle, her jeans at the other side of the room and her knickers pulled down to her knees. Seeing that her friend was naked and unconscious next to her, she rushed out of the flat and raised the alarm. It had been sixteen hours since they had first entered Peter Tobin's flat.

By the time the police arrived and found the second girl still unconscious, Tobin was long gone. As he would do thirteen years later, after murdering Angelika Kluk, he adopted a pseudonym in a bid to stay one step ahead of the police. A witness soon came forward to say that they had seen Tobin heading towards Brighton, and all the south coast ports were alerted in the hope that Tobin might get careless or even hand himself in once he ran out of money. But the trail soon went cold. No sooner had Tobin arrived in Brighton than he found refuge among a Christian group on a day trip from the Jesus

Fellowship Church in Warwickshire. Using his estranged wife's maiden name, Peter 'Wilson' was invited back to the secluded King's House Centre, near Southam, after claiming he was homeless. In return for their charity, he promised to do odd jobs around the country house.

Eventually, however, Tobin's new friends grew suspicious about his background. Around a month later, he was asked to leave. Tobin, by now sporting a moustache, did as they asked. Days later, members of the Christian group were watching the BBC's *Crimewatch* when they saw the face of the man they knew as Peter Wilson. They immediately contacted the police, and a few days later Tobin was found in Brighton and arrested. On 18 May 1994, at Winchester Crown Court, he was sentenced to fourteen years' imprisonment for his sadistic attack on the two girls. Anthony Davies, prosecuting, observed: 'Tobin treated the girls as cruelly as a cat would treat a mouse.'

In 2001, after serving just seven years, Tobin was released on licence. However, he breached the terms of the licence soon after being released – he failed to inform the police of his whereabouts – and once he was found he was sent back to prison for another three years. Placed on the sex offenders register, Tobin was again released on licence on 18 May 2004. Just over two years later, using the pseudonym Pat McLaughlin, he would murder Angelika Kluk.

The surname he chose on that occasion bore a close resemblance to that of a woman he had befriended in Paisley between 2004 and 2005. But their friendship did not last long, because Cheryl McLachlan only narrowly escaped becoming another of Peter Tobin's victims.

October 2005

Cheryl raised a faint smile when she saw Tobin in the street in Paisley. He was a drinking buddy of the guy she was seeing. She thought of him as a kind old gent, not unlike her father, who had died a couple of years before. He was never sleazy, there were no innuendoes, he was always charming, and they shared an interest in football. Cheryl had used to play herself, and she had worked as a stadium steward. There was a live match on TV later, so Tobin asked if she fancied watching the game in a pub. Alternatively, they could go back to his place, where they could also have a decent cup of coffee. It wouldn't be the first time that Cheryl had been to Tobin's flat – she'd popped in once or twice for a cigarette and a chat – so she agreed and the pair of them walked to his home.

Twenty-four-year-old Cheryl hadn't been there long before she noticed that Tobin was restless, even a little agitated. He kept walking in and out of the living room, rather than taking it easy and putting his feet up to watch the match. She couldn't enjoy the game herself, so she decided to leave him to it. 'That's me off. Thanks for the coffee,' she shouted from the lounge while he was in the kitchen. There was no reply, but within a moment Tobin rushed into the lounge holding a knife. Spittle flew out of his mouth as he yelled at her to lie down on the sofa. Cheryl struggled, but Tobin forced her back and then threw all of his weight on top of her. The gentle man she had grown to like had been transformed into a knife-wielding maniac. As Tobin lifted the knife to her neck, Cheryl thought she was about to die. In a desperate bid to survive, she pushed against Tobin with all her might. Off balance, he fell to the floor and landed on the base of his spine. This gave

Cheryl time to get off the sofa and head towards the front door.

But she didn't leave quietly. 'What the hell are you playing at? Put that knife down!' she screamed as she made for the exit.

Then Tobin came at her again. However, he didn't have the element of surprise this time, so Cheryl managed to grab the hand that was holding the knife. They wrestled and fell back onto the sofa. As the cushions scattered to the floor, Cheryl caught sight of a belt and a tie that had been concealed underneath them. She was sure they would have been used either to tie her up or to strangle her. By now more furious than terrified, she reached for the knife with her free hand. The adrenalin flowing through her body meant she felt no pain as the blade sliced open her palm. Again fighting free from Tobin, she shouted for help as she raced for the door, only to reach it and find it locked. Looking over her shoulder, she saw Tobin running at her yet again. The key was in the door, but it fell to the floor as she tried to turn it. With no other option, she turned and faced her attacker, convinced he was about to stab her to death.

'Put that thing down and let me out of here. Or else!' The words exploded out of Cheryl's mouth.

To her amazement, Tobin stopped in his tracks. The fury seemed to ebb from him and he placed the knife on the floor. Then he staggered back into the lounge, his hand on his heart, apologising as he went. 'Cheryl, I'm sorry,' he said. 'I was joking. I got carried away. I didn't mean any harm. I'm just a daft old boy. I've near enough given myself a heart attack.'

It will be remembered that Tobin had been admitted to

hospital with abdominal pains after murdering Vicky Hamilton, and in 2006 he would seek help for chest pains after murdering Angelika Kluk. So a vicious attack followed by a pathetic search for sympathy for *his* physical problems was obviously a pattern with Tobin. And Cheryl *was* sympathetic: she found his medicine and handed it to him before leaving. Only then did she contact the police. By the time they arrived at his flat, though, Tobin had made a miraculous recovery and had left.

Now calling himself Pat McLaughlin, he again found refuge in a religious community, just as he had after attacking the two schoolgirls in Portsmouth. This time, though, it was Catholic rather than evangelical – St Patrick's church in Anderston. A few months later, he would claim his final victim: Angelika Kluk.

But Cheryl McLachlan still had a role to play in his life. When the police announced that they wanted to speak to the handyman who had fled the church so abruptly following Angelika's disappearance, the TV report broadcast a picture of a man they were calling Pat McLaughlin. That picture sent a shiver down Cheryl's spine, because she knew that the police had the wrong name. She picked up the phone and told them that the man they wanted was not Pat McLaughlin, but Peter Tobin. And that he had tried to kill her almost exactly a year before.

Chapter Nine

Cold Cases

> 'I have never yet been beaten,' said the hare, boasting.
> 'When I put forth my full speed, I challenge anyone
> here to race with me.'
>
> 'I accept your challenge,' the tortoise said quietly.
>
> 'That is a good joke,' said the hare. 'I could dance
> round you all the way.'
>
> 'Keep your boasting till you've beaten me,'
> answered the tortoise. 'Shall we race?'
>
> 'The Tortoise and the Hare', *Aesop's Fables*

Peter Tobin danced around the police for most of his life. Aged seven, he was sent to an approved school. Later, he would 'graduate' to a young offenders' institution. Burglary, forgery and conspiracy would in time land him short jail sentences. Despite his arrest and conviction in 1994, and the ten years he subsequently spent in prison, he must have thought he'd put one over the police, because at that point they still had no idea that he was responsible for the deaths of Vicky Hamilton and Dinah McNicol. Even in 2007, following his conviction for the murder of Angelika Kluk and his arrest in prison for the murders of Vicky and Dinah, he still believed he was ahead of the game. He protested that he knew nothing of the two girls and pleaded not guilty to both murder charges. Just like the hare in Aesop's fable, Tobin thought he could never be beaten. But advances in forensic science technology and DNA profiling would eventually wipe the smug smile from his face. As Judge Lord Emslie said in his closing remarks at Tobin's trial for the murder of Vicky Hamilton: 'This was a vulnerable teenager who needed help on her way home but instead, she fell into your clutches and you brought her short life to an end in a disgusting and degrading way. Yet again, you have shown yourself to be unfit to live in decent society.'

Tobin used his freedom to fulfil his evil fantasies and sexual desires year on year. So it was little wonder that once the true horror of Tobin's crimes became clear, police forces with cold cases on their books from the last forty years began to re-examine some of their most notorious unsolved murders. Such were his itinerant lifestyle and the police's initial inability to pin down exactly where he had lived for many years that suspicions grew that he could be implicated in any number of murders. After all, he had plenty of form. Being the subject of a police investigation and standing before a judge were nothing new for him.

Tobin Timeline

1960–65	Worked in the Strathclyde area
Late 1969–70	Worked in the Sussex area
Early 1970	Worked in the Strathclyde area
1970–73	Imprisoned
Mid-1970s	Worked in the Sussex area as a labourer, then in Strathclyde as a driver
Late 1970s	Worked in the Sussex area
1977–78	Possibly lived in or visited Glasgow
1980s	Worked as a caretaker in Sussex
January–July 1984	Imprisoned
1985–86	Whereabouts unknown
1986–90	Worked in Brighton, then moved to Bathgate
1991	Moved from Bathgate to Margate
1993	Worked in Havant, Hampshire
1994–2004	Imprisoned
2005	Worked in Paisley
2006–	Imprisoned

When Lord Emslie sentenced Tobin at the end of the Vicky Hamilton murder trial, he echoed the words of Detective Inspector Andy Stewart, who in 1994 had described Tobin's attack on the two schoolgirls in Havant: 'Tobin has committed a despicable act and he has been sentenced for that act. I doubt they [the children] will ever come to terms with what has happened to them. In my experience I have never come across

a case that has appalled me so much.' Tragically, Tobin was
freed after serving only ten years for that 'despicable act', which
gave him the opportunity to kill again just two years later. But
as the timeline of his adult life indicates, he was also free for the
vast majority of the 1960s, 1970s and 1980s, and for half of the
1990s. During each of his three brief marriages, most of his
appalling behaviour seems to have been directed at his wife.
But what of when he was single? Did he attack other women in
those periods? And if he did, when did his killing begin?

Serial Killer, but How Prolific?

We can label Peter Tobin a 'serial killer' because we know that
he killed at least three people – Vicky Hamilton, Dinah
McNicol and Angelika Kluk – over a considerable period of
time. (This definition differentiates serial killers from 'spree
murderers', who may kill just as many people, but do so in the
course of one incident. An example of the latter is Michael
Ryan, who murdered sixteen people in Hungerford in 1987.)
But every serial killer has been suspected of killing more victims than has been proved in a court of law. Even Harold
Shipman – Britain's most prolific serial killer, who is known to
have murdered 215 people – is suspected of having killed
another 45.

So how many unsolved crimes might be attributed to Peter
Tobin? As the details of his offending were shared among
police forces, debated by journalists and discussed by the
public, his name began to be connected to some of the country's most notorious murders. Among them, of course, were the
three committed by Bible John in 1968 and 1969. But newspaper articles and TV reports have speculated about his

involvement in at least another twelve murders committed
during the 1970s and 1980s. In truth, though, it is unlikely that
Tobin was involved in any of these later crimes. After all, he
wasn't the only serial killer (let alone the only murderer)
around in the 1970s and 1980s, so holding him responsible for
almost every unsolved murder committed in those decades
is somewhat far-fetched. To illustrate our point, we provide
a few examples below. It is worth noting here that although
viable DNA samples in some cases would appear to make ruling
Tobin in or out of some of these crimes a simple process, the
police force's primary focus remains, quite rightly, 'live' cases. It
can take some time for cold cases such as these to be thoroughly
re-investigated, even when links have been suggested. As
such it is difficult to reach definitive conclusions about Tobin's
involvement, or even – in some cases – to know how far the
police have pursued the investigation.

Big Hairy Monster

May 1994 was a good month for the safety of women and girls
in Britain. Peter Tobin was sent down for fourteen years at
Winchester Crown Court, while at Newcastle Crown Court a
delivery van driver was given a minimum term of thirty-five
years for the abduction and sexual assault of four young girls,
and the murder of three of them. As the balding, powerful
figure of forty-seven-year-old Robert Black was led from the
dock and down to the cells to begin his ten life sentences, he
paused, glanced coldly at the officers from six forces who had
spent twelve years hunting him down, and said: 'Well done,
boys.' Moments later, he was calmly pacing up and down his
cell in silence, sipping tea, seemingly unfazed by being

branded the most sadistic child killer since Myra Hindley and Ian Brady.

Rejected by his natural mother within days of his birth in April 1947 in Grangemouth, Black was soon fostered by a West Highlands couple, Jack and Margaret Tulip. 'Smelly Robbie Tulip', as he was known at school, developed an interest in sex at an early age, comparing his genitalia with those of a girl when he was aged just five. By the age of eleven, both of his foster parents had died, so Black was placed in care at the Redding Children's Home, near Falkirk. He was already fascinated by vaginas and anuses, and the following year he made his first attempt at rape. He and two other boys took a girl from the children's home to a nearby field, where they forcibly removed the girl's knickers, lifted her skirt and attempted penetration. With all three boys failing to have intercourse, they contented themselves with touching the girl's vagina. The incident was eventually uncovered, and Black was moved to a stricter, all-boy institution in Musselburgh. While there, until the age of fifteen, he was regularly sexually abused by a male member of staff. But soon he was able to leave, and with help from the authorities he managed to get a job as a delivery boy in and around Glasgow. During his rounds, he molested up to forty girls. None of these incidents was reported at the time. By his late teens, Black was committing the kind of act that would typify the rest of his criminal life. At seventeen, he approached a seven-year-old girl in a park and asked her if she wanted to see some kittens. He led the trusting child to a disused building, choked her until she fell unconscious, raped her, then left her alone in the building. The girl was later found wandering the streets confused, crying and bleeding, but she was subsequently able to identify her attacker. However, when the case came to court, Black received nothing more than a ticking off and a warning to behave in the future.

By his twenties, he had moved to London, where his interest in swimming landed him a job as a lifeguard. From his perch at the side of the pool, he would stare at young girls in their bathing suits. Often, though, merely looking wasn't enough to satisfy his sexual urges. At least one official complaint of indecent behaviour was made against him, but Black was never charged. He did eventually lose his job, however.

Towards the end of his twenties, Black began working for a company called Poster Dispatch and Storage, a job that allowed him to travel all over the UK for fifteen years. One of his regular runs was between London and Scotland. A few years later, young girls who lived on that route started to disappear.

In July 1982, eleven-year-old Susan Maxwell was abducted as she returned home to her farmhouse in the small village of Cornhill on Tweed, on the English side of the border with Scotland. Her body was discovered two weeks later – 250 miles away in a ditch next to a lay-by on the A518, just outside Uttoxeter in the Midlands. Almost exactly a year later, five-year-old Caroline Hogg was abducted from the Scottish seaside resort of Portobello. Ten days later, her body was found in a lay-by at Twycross, close to the road running between Coventry and Northampton – nearly 300 miles from where she had disappeared. Three years later, in 1986, there was another abduction. Ten-year-old Sarah Harper was abducted in Morley, Leeds. Three weeks later, her body was discovered floating in the River Trent. Police were convinced that she had been put in the river near Junction 24 of the M1.

All three victims had been abducted from public locations, sexually assaulted, driven south, murdered and dumped in the Midlands, all within twenty-six miles of each other. Police were sure this was the work of one man, but they had to wait four more years before making a breakthrough.

It was a sunny day in July 1990 and retired shopkeeper David Herkes was outside his home in Stow, in the Scottish Borders, determined to take advantage of the good weather and cut his lawn. Walking along the other side of the road, on her way to a friend's house to play, was a six-year-old girl, who began approaching a van with its passenger door open. As Mr Herkes stooped over to inspect his lawnmower blades, he could make out the feet of his young neighbour beneath the van. But he could also see those of a man, standing next to her. Suddenly her feet vanished, and Mr Herkes saw the man leaning in towards the van's dashboard, as if shoving something into the footwell. As the van pulled away, she was nowhere to be seen. Realising she had been snatched, Mr Herkes made a quick mental note of the van's registration number, raced into his house and rang the police.

While officers searched the area, Black put the terrified young girl through an appalling sexual assault in a nearby quarry. However, unaware that he'd been spotted abducting the six-year-old, Black later doubled back through the village. David Herkes recalls: 'I was standing near the spot where the child had been abducted, briefing the police and the girl's distraught father about what had happened. Suddenly I saw the van again and shouted, "That's him." The officer dashed into the road and the van swerved to avoid him before coming to a halt.'

It was the girl's father, himself a police officer, who opened the van door to find her among a pile of rags behind the seat. She had been shoved into a sleeping-bag which had been zipped closed. Her hands had been tied behind her back, and her mouth taped shut with Elastoplast. Such was the temperature that day that police believe she would almost certainly have suffocated had she remained in the sleeping-bag for much longer.

Black was sentenced to life imprisonment for this crime at the High Court in Edinburgh later that year. Then, in 1994, he was found guilty of the murders of Susan Maxwell, Caroline Hogg and Sarah Harper, thanks in part to the presentation of 'evidence of similar fact' at the trial. In what was an unusual move by a British court at the time, the prosecution was granted permission to show the jury evidence of other abductions Black had committed. In addition, and crucially, Black's credit card receipts from petrol stations and the delivery notes from the poster companies to which he delivered proved that he was in the vicinity of the kidnap locations when the three girls were abducted.

As a child, Robert Black had nightmares about a 'big hairy monster' under his bed. He became that monster, but after 1994, unlike Peter Tobin, Black would never walk free again.

Beside the Seaside, Beside the Sea

Tobin liked to be beside the seaside. If he wasn't in his native Scotland, he was usually on the south coast, near Brighton or Portsmouth. Generally, after the late 1960s, he moved back north of the border only because it was no longer safe for him to be south of it (and vice versa). Then, once things had cooled off, and often under a pseudonym, he would be on the move again. But there was one place to which he kept returning – Norfolk. For Tobin, there was nothing better than getting away from it all and taking a holiday in the East Anglian county. It had pretty villages and coastal market towns as well as the Broads, with their miles of waterways. It also appealed to him because he never stayed long enough to become well known. Anonymity was vitally important for Tobin – he might be in the community, but he was never really part of it. He knew what he might do at any time, but to everyone else in Norfolk he was just another holidaymaker. And before anyone got too close, he would be off, not to return perhaps until the next bank holiday.

This connection to Norfolk is one reason why the county's police force started to re-examine cold cases of the missing and the murdered there over the past forty years. It was hoped that one or more of them could ultimately be traced back to Tobin, and indeed several of them were soon found to contain his hallmarks. The oldest case that Norfolk Constabulary re-investigated dated back to 1969, which made it one of Britain's longest-running missing person inquiries – the disappearance of April Fabb on 8 April that year. It will be noticed that this date falls between the first and second Bible John murders.

It should have taken April only a matter of minutes to cycle the two miles along the country lane from her home in Metton, near Cromer, to her sister's house in Roughton. The thirteen-year-old wanted to deliver a packet of cigarettes to her brother-in-law for his birthday. Forty years later, the school-girl's family still do not know what happened to her. April's bicycle was discovered by the side of the road in a field, but she was nowhere to be seen. The presumed abduction sparked the largest police investigation Norfolk had ever seen, and over the decades the Major Investigation Team regularly explored new leads and tip-offs. Of course, the case strongly resembles the abductions committed by Robert Black. But this time there was nothing to link Black to the scene of the crime – no delivery records, no petrol station receipts.

However, the Norfolk coast was a known haunt of Peter Tobin. And twenty-five years later he would be convicted for the sexual assault of two girls who were only a little older than April. We also know that Tobin was an opportunist mur-derer, a born liar who was able to kill and then act as if nothing had happened. He hadn't planned to pick up Dinah McNicol in 1991 – he had just spotted her waiting at the side of the road and had taken advantage of the fact. Nor could he have known that Vicky Hamilton would be waiting at the bus stop in Bathgate, yet he acted quickly once he saw her there. A young girl running a birthday errand on her bike might have proved equally irresistible to him. Furthermore, the abduction took place the day after Easter Monday, which fitted with Tobin's habit of taking bank holiday breaks in Norfolk.

Just a year after April had gone missing, Norfolk Constabu-lary were dealing not with a missing person inquiry but with a murder. This time, the culprit had casually left the body in a quiet street for the police to find. So the crime took place just a few months after the third and final Bible John murder, and the victim's body was abandoned in a startlingly similar way to those of Pat Docker, Mima McDonald and Helen Puttock.

On the night of 10 March 1970, eighteen-year-old insurance worker Susan Long had met up with her boyfriend Brian Tingate in Norwich for an evening's dancing at the Gala Ballroom. But it was a work night – Tuesday – so she couldn't stay out too long. After leaving the ballroom, she caught the bus to Aylsham and arrived at the small town just after 11 p.m. A witness saw her getting off the bus in Aylsham's Market Place. She appeared to be alone. Then it should have been just a seven-minute walk home. However, at some point on that walk, Susan was dragged into a secluded 'lovers' lane', raped, strangled with the straps of her own handbag, and tossed into a puddle. By the early hours of the morning, her parents had raised the alarm. A few hours later, while it was still dark, her body was found by a milkman on his early morning delivery round.

The killer left traces of his blood on Susan's clothes, but despite this and an extensive investigation at the time, he was never caught. However, thirty-four years later, detectives reopened the case in light of developments in DNA analysis. Tests were conducted on the blood found on Susan's clothing, and a forensics team was able to create a DNA profile of the murderer. The local police then revisited a number of people who had been questioned during the original investigation. But perhaps the killer had not lived locally. Perhaps he had merely been on holiday in the area – as Peter Tobin was on numerous occasions.

Of course, we know that Bible John found his three victims at a dancehall, and they were also exploited by Peter Tobin when he was looking for vulnerable young women – he first met both Margaret Mackintosh and Cathy Wilson at a ball-room. Bible John would also drag his victims into secluded alleys before strangling them. So was Susan Long Bible John's fourth victim? The timing was certainly right, just four months after Helen Puttock's murder, but what of the location? Had Bible John left Glasgow to allow things to cool off a little? Had he headed to Norfolk, a popular holiday destination, to lie low? It has always seemed strange that the Bible John killings sud-denly stopped in October 1969. But perhaps they did not. Perhaps the murderer simply took his hunger for killing else-where. Susan's killer is still to be brought to justice, so the case remains open.

Among the other cases Norfolk Constabulary re-investigated was that of a headless woman's body discovered in weeds by the side of Cley Road in Cockley Cley, near Swaffham, in 1974. She was wearing a pink, frilly Marks and Spencer nightdress and her trussed-up body – her arms and legs had been bound to her torso – was wrapped in brown plastic sheeting bearing the initials 'NCR'. The woman's head was never found and she has never been identified. Police could merely guess that she was aged between twenty-three and thirty-five and that her body was dumped in early August. An extensive police inves-tigation in which 700 statements were taken and 15,000 people were questioned initially seemed to produce some quite good leads. For instance, the plastic sheeting was traced to a Scottish company called National Cash Register, and detectives learned that the firm made only six such sheets between 1962 and 1968. However, at the time, this line of enquiry led nowhere, and the case was wound up in 1975.

Thirty years later, though, it was deemed worthy of re-examination for several very good reasons. Peter Tobin was living in Glasgow between 1962 and 1968, so he could well have acquired one of those six plastic sheets. Later, of course, he would use plastic sheeting to wrap up the bodies of Vicky Hamilton and Dinah McNicol as well as to hide Angelika Kluk when he moved her from the garage into the church. And he was not squeamish about using a knife on his victims, as his dissection of Vicky proved. Finally, Dinah's arms and legs were bound in a very similar way to those of the unknown woman found in Cockley Cley.

After studying Tobin's modus operandi, Norfolk's Major Investigation Team exhumed the remains of the unidentified woman in the hope that new DNA analysis techniques would allow them to identify her, her killer, or both. Home Office pathologist Dr Nat Carey carried out a second post-mortem examination on the corpse, while a forensic anthropologist from Cambridge University studied her bones and the rest of her remains. However, neither man was able to find anything conclusive and eventually the victim was reinterred. Her identity and that of the person who killed her remain mysteries.

Just days after the county of Norfolk had been forced to deal with the gruesome discovery of a headless woman, another young woman disappeared.

Twenty-one-year-old Pamela Exall was staying at the Dinglea Campsite in Snettisham, just twenty miles from Cockley Cley. She had recently qualified from Kingston Polytechnic and was hoping to take up a job as an articled clerk with Berkshire County Council, but it was still the summer and there was fun to be had, so she, her brother Peter and their friend

David had embarked on a motorcycling holiday. It was Friday, 30 August when they arrived at the campsite, the last stop on their break before they started to make their way back home. After a meal and a few drinks, they stopped at a phone box near the sailing club. Pamela called her mother and father in Fleet, Hampshire, to tell them she was having a lovely holiday but would be home on Sunday evening, even though it was a bank holiday weekend. The boys then decided to head back to the campsite, while Pamela set out alone in the direction of the beach for a moonlit stroll. She was wearing blue jeans, a black leather jacket and brown suede shoes. It was 10.30 p.m. That was the last time anyone saw her alive. The two boys didn't know she was missing until the next morning, when they checked her tent. All her possessions were there, but there was no sign of Pamela.

For the fourth time in five years, the Norfolk Constabulary found themselves trying to find out what had happened to a young woman in their normally peaceful community. This time, they searched the mud-flats of the Wash and the lake at the nearby bird sanctuary, but they found nothing. Comparisons have been drawn between Pamela's disappearance and that of Dinah McNicol in 1991, and Tobin's former wives have been contacted by the police in a bid to find out precisely where and when he holidayed in Norfolk. So far, though, they have uncovered no evidence to link Tobin with Pamela's abduction, and once again the case remains open.

Jumping forward a number of years, but still in Norfolk, another case that continues to baffle investigators is that of fourteen-year-old Johanna Young.

At 7.30 p.m. on 23 December 1992, Johanna left her house

on Merton Road, Watton, and headed towards her local fish and chip shop. She was seen outside the shop half an hour later. But when she didn't return home, and having phoned round all of Johanna's friends, her parents raised the alarm. On Boxing Day, her semi-naked body was discovered just four hundred yards from her home, in a water-filled pit on the edge of Wayland Wood. This was barely eight miles from where the body of the headless woman had been found fourteen years earlier. A post-mortem established that, despite suffering a fractured skull and being unconscious, Johanna had still been alive when her killer had dumped her body. She had died by drowning. Hampered by a lack of scientific evidence, the seventy officers assigned to the investigation were never able to bring the schoolgirl's murderer to justice.

The crime took place the year after Tobin murdered and buried the bodies of Vicky Hamilton and Dinah McNicol. Did Tobin return to Norfolk that Christmas to kill yet again?

Itinerant Evil – 1970

Because Peter Tobin travelled between the south coast of England and southern Scotland so regularly – not to mention his many excursions to Norfolk – police can rarely discount him when they look again at cases of women who were murdered on or near those routes.

On Sunday, 8 March 1970, Jackie Ansell Lamb decided to hitch-hike from London to Manchester. She must have thought she had picked a good day to catch a lift. On the Saturday, Manchester City had played West Bromwich Albion in the League Cup Final at Wembley, so many of the fans were heading back up to the Midlands and the North-West. Jackie was wearing a blond wig, false eyelashes, a dark blue coat and maroon patent-leather shoes, and a woman matching that description was seen getting into a car at Keele services between 4 and 5 p.m. But Jackie never arrived home. Six days later, in a wood near Knutsford, Cheshire, the eighteen-year-old's sexually assaulted body was discovered by a farmer. She had been strangled. In their investigation, the police distributed four thousand posters appealing for help, but they never found Jackie's murderer.

Of course, Peter Tobin picked up Dinah McNicol when she was hitch-hiking twenty-one years later, so he has a record of this kind of crime. But if Tobin did kill Jackie, and then murdered Susan Long, he must have driven from Cheshire to Norfolk almost immediately, because the two crimes were committed only two days apart.

In October that year another hitch-hiker was murdered. The semi-naked body of twenty-four-year-old Barbara Mayo was found by walkers in woodland in Derbyshire, near the M1, six days after she had gone missing. She had been raped, repeatedly punched around the head and strangled with a length of flex – all hallmarks of a Tobin murder.

As we know, DNA profiling was in its infancy in 1970, but twenty years later the police were able to test samples taken from Jackie and Barbara. They concluded that the two women were killed by the same person. Two hundred and fifty known sex offenders and other offenders were traced and tested, but no matches were found and no arrests were made. Soon, though, the DNA samples taken from the two victims would be cross-referenced with Peter Tobin's profile.

Genette Tate, Suzanne Lawrence, Jessie Earl and Pamela Hastie

Thirteen-year-old Genette Tate, fourteen-year-old Suzanne Lawrence and twenty-two-year-old Jessie Earl were murdered over a two-year period, beginning in 1978. Peter Tobin's second marriage had ended by then, and he wouldn't meet his third wife until 1986. Little is known of his whereabouts or indeed his state of mind between those two marriages, but we can speculate that he would have been an angry and frustrated man. Sylvia Jefferies had managed to escape from him, and she had taken his only son with her. For someone as obsessed with power and control as Tobin, that must have been a very bitter pill to swallow.

So, Peter Tobin was at liberty, he had no wife to abuse, and he was almost certainly holding a profound grudge against women. However, there is an alternative suspect for these three murders. By 1978, Robert Black had been on the road as a delivery driver for two years, yet his first known murder victim is Susan Maxwell, whom he killed in July 1982. Is it possible that Black struck before then?

As twelve-year-old Maggie Heavey and her friend Tracey Pratt walked together through the small village of Aylesbeare, near Exeter, with the late afternoon August sun beating down on the narrow hedge-lined lanes, they saw Ginny cycling towards them, laden down with newspapers on her weekend round. Her full name was Genette, but all her friends called her Ginny. Tracey knew Ginny would be pedalling past her house in a short while, so she decided to intercept her parents' delivery. With no time to waste, Ginny set off once more and pedalled around the corner to her next drop-off point. Maggie and Tracey sat down briefly on the grass verge and flicked through the paper, paying particular attention to a story about a UFO sighting in the area. Before long, they were ambling towards the corner Ginny had rounded just a few minutes earlier. Then they saw Ginny's bike on the ground, its back wheel still spinning, newspapers strewn across the tarmac. The two girls shouted for their friend to come out, thinking she must be hiding from them. But their calls were never answered. Collecting up the newspapers, Maggie wheeled the bicycle back home and told her mother of Ginny's disappearance. Soon Genette Tate would be front-page news on the very papers she had delivered. The media besieged the village and looked for leads, while hundreds of local residents and numerous others scoured the surrounding countryside for anything that might help the police.

But more than thirty years later, Ginny's whereabouts remain a mystery. Since her disappearance, a mountain of paperwork relating to the case has piled up inside a ten-by-twelve-foot cage at Devon and Cornwall Police's headquarters. Also under lock and key is Ginny's bike, which has been subjected to countless examinations by forensic experts. So far, one man has remained the central focus of the investigation – Robert Black. All of his known victims were abducted from public places, and he even admitted that he specifically targeted girls on paper rounds. Furthermore, his work records and petrol station receipts indicate that he might have been in the area when Ginny disappeared. And one eyewitness even claimed to have seen him near Exeter airport. However, when Devon and Cornwall Police interviewed Black in 1996, he denied any involvement in Ginny's disappearance, and his position remained unchanged when he was re-interviewed two years later. In 2002 detectives revisited the cold case yet again, and within a year they thought they'd made a minor breakthrough. Police scientists managed to recover Ginny's DNA profile from one of her jumpers, which her mother had kept ever since her disappearance. But so far they have been unable to discover a matching profile while investigating potential suspects. Nevertheless, three years later, Devon and Cornwall Police sent the case file to the Crown Prosecution Service, in the hope of starting proceedings against Black. The CPS concluded that there was insufficient evidence to bring him to trial.

In some interviews, Ginny's father has said that his daughter bore a 'striking' resemblance to Dinah McNicol, but there is no evidence to link Tobin to the Devon girl's disappearance. The case remains open.

Another schoolgirl vanished less than a year after Ginny, but from the other side of the country. Suzanne Lawrence disappeared from Romford, Essex, in July 1979. She had been visiting her sister in Harold Hill, and as she left she said: 'Tell Mum I'll be home later this evening.' But she never made it home, in much the same way as Vicky Hamilton and Dinah McNicol would fail to reach their destinations twelve years later.

In all likelihood, Peter Tobin was still living on the south coast of England in 1979. But he would continue to visit Norfolk, especially during the summer. To get there and back, he would almost certainly have joined the A12 at Harold Hill. However, this was also a well-trodden route back into London for Robert Black after his delivery trips. Again, the abduction itself bears all the hallmarks of a Black attack, so he has been the prime suspect for many years. However, he has never been charged over it. And now, given Tobin's connection with the area, the police must at least consider the possibility that he was the perpetrator.

Meanwhile, detectives in Sussex, the county where Tobin lived and worked for most of the late 1970s and early 1980s, have also been re-examining a number of their cold cases in the hope of finding a link to Britain's newest serial killer. Top of their list is the case of a young woman who vanished in 1980.

Jessie Earl was a strong and independent Londoner. She was in her second year studying graphics at Eastbourne College of Art and Design, and there was no place she'd rather be. Inspired by the Sussex coast, she loved to write about and be among nature, with a particular favourite being a long walk on Beachy Head. On Wednesday 15 May, she rang home from a phone box on the seafront to tell her mother she would see her on Friday. Eastbourne's mainline station was just a two- or three-minute walk through a park from Jessie's bedsit – which was one of the reasons why she was so fond of her place in Upperton Gardens.

When Jessie failed to arrive on Friday, her parents, John and Valerie, were not overly concerned that she hadn't shown up. But they *were* worried that she hadn't phoned to tell them that she'd changed her plans. She was a conscientious girl and always let them know if she was going to be late. Valerie caught the train down to Eastbourne the following day to try to find out what had happened. Upon opening the door to her daughter's bedsit, she instantly and instinctively knew that something was wrong. There were dirty dinner dishes on the table, a book and Jessie's reading glasses on the floor and her purse on the bed. The room seemed to have been abandoned – as if Jessie had just popped out for a minute, but had never returned. Valerie immediately picked up the phone and called her husband. Later, some of Jessie's friends told Valerie they thought she was back in London for the weekend. Others said they had seen her in the days running up to Wednesday, but not since then.

Jessie's disappearance triggered a full-scale missing person inquiry. Police helicopters and sniffer dogs swept the area, and her bedsit was searched for clues. Meanwhile, John and Valerie produced three thousand missing person posters, which were displayed all over the country. But every trail the police followed soon reached a dead end, and the investigation was eventually scaled down.

The Earls never gave up hope their daughter would be found. In time they even made appearances on the BBC's *Wogan* chat show and *Crimewatch* to appeal for information. Then, in 1989, seemingly out of the blue, John and Valerie received a visit from the police. An eight-year-old girl had been flying her kite on Beachy Head before losing control of it in the gusty wind. The kite had ploughed into an overgrown thicket, and when the child's father had waded into the undergrowth to retrieve it he had made a gruesome discovery. First, he had seen the skull, then the rest of the bones. He had discovered the remains of Jessie Earl, nine years after she had disappeared. The only piece of clothing the police found was a bra, tied in a knot around Jessie's wrists. There was no sign of her silver ring, her watch, her leather bag or even her asthma inhaler. But all forensics could establish was that Jessie had died at the scene, one of her favourite places.

Yet again, though, police hoped that advances in DNA analysis techniques might eventually lead them to the killer. A squad of fourteen officers cleared an area of some twenty square yards around where the skeleton had been found, and this was then excavated, with the soil minutely examined for evidence. A forensic archaeologist, assisted by thirty volunteers from a metal detector club, also combed the clifftop. They uncovered dozens of items, including belt buckles and jewellery, but none of them helped the investigation. The case review was finally closed in 2000. The Eastbourne Coroner recorded an open verdict because he said there was a lack of evidence that might have proved a cause of death.

However, since the discovery of the bodies of Vicky Hamilton and Dinah McNicol in Tobin's former house in Margate, police have returned to the home of John and Valerie Earl to take DNA samples from them and from Jessie's clothing, hoping to find a match with any of Tobin's clothes or possessions. Tobin was living just twenty-five miles from Eastbourne, in Brighton, when Jessie vanished. Perhaps even more significantly, hospital records show that he was back in Glasgow shortly thereafter. As we have seen, Tobin had a habit of moving as far away as possible after committing a murder. Sussex Police also learned that Tobin used Vicky Hamilton's bra to tie her up. So far, though, none of these similarities has led to any firm evidence that would enable police to charge Tobin with the murder of Jessie Earl.

In 1981 sixteen-year-old schoolgirl Pamela Hastie was

raped, strangled and dumped in Rannoch Woods in Johnstone, Renfrewshire – the town where Peter Tobin was born. The following year another Johnstone man, Raymond Gilmour, was convicted of Pamela's murder and sentenced to life, despite a lack of forensic evidence linking him to either her or the crime scene. Gilmour protested his innocence throughout his trial and subsequent prison term, claiming that a confession had been beaten out of him by the police. He was released in 2002 after serving twenty-one years. His conviction was finally quashed in 2007. Peter Tobin is now being investigated for Pamela's murder.

Police are also re-investigating the death of another Renfrewshire woman, Dorothea Meechan, whose strangled body was found dumped in bushes in 1971. Former neighbours of Tobin, who has lived in both Paisley and Renfrew, to the west of Glasgow, have been re-interviewed and questioned by police.

However, geographical proximity to the scene of a historic crime, even if it can be established, does not automatically make Tobin the murderer. The 'babes in the wood' case demonstrates that all too well.

Thursday, 9 October 1986

Close friends Karen Hadaway and Nicola Fellows were barely half a mile from their homes on the Moulsecombe council estate when they stopped at the Seafare fish and chip shop on the Barcombe Road, on the outskirts of Brighton. It was the last time anyone but their killer saw the two nine-year-olds alive. Once they failed to return home, a huge police search was launched. Soon people from the estate were flooding into the local streets and parks to look for the girls. Then, at 4.15 p.m. the following day, their bodies were discovered together, hidden in bushes in Wild Park, opposite the estate. Lying in mud, partially clothed, one girl was lying at an angle with her arm across her friend's chest. Nicola's lips were speckled with blood. Both girls had been raped and strangled. The investigation that followed was the largest in Sussex Police's history. Peter Tobin was living in Brighton at the time, but to the local police he was seen merely as an occasional petty criminal. Instead, another man rapidly became the lead suspect.

Twenty-year-old Russell Bishop was himself a petty criminal with several convictions for burglary. However, he was also a friend and former lodger of the Hadaway family. When Karen's parents were going out, they often asked Bishop to babysit. Bishop joined the search as soon as news of the girls' disappearance spread around the estate, and then contacted the police to say that he had found their bodies. He provided detailed descriptions of what he'd seen when he'd pulled back the bushes to reveal the two girls, and maintained that he had tried to find a pulse on both of them. However, after recording all of this evidence and recovering the two girls' bodies from exactly the spot indicated by Bishop, officers on the ground started to compare notes. It transpired that the area where the girls were found had been cordoned off as soon as the search had begun, so Bishop could not have got close enough to see anything, let alone try to find a pulse.

Bishop's girlfriend then came forward to say a sweatshirt found near the scene belonged to him. He denied it, claiming he had been on the campus of Sussex University at the time of the girls' disappearance, trying to break into cars. Next he said he made up the story about finding the girls because he wanted people to think he was a hero. He tried to explain the accuracy of his description of the scene by saying he had simply guessed how the girls would be found.

On the final day of Bishop's trial, the jury took barely two hours to find him not guilty – they had not been convinced that the sweatshirt belonged to Bishop. Bishop then appealed for witnesses to come forward so that the 'real killer' could be brought to justice. However, within four years, he was in jail, having been convicted in a case that bore startling comparison with the 'babes in the wood' murders. In 1990, he bundled a seven-year-old girl into the boot of his car, assaulted her and left her for dead on Devil's Dyke, on the Sussex Downs. But the naked girl managed to stagger onto a nearby road, where she pleaded with a passer-by to save her from the 'bad man'. Remarkably, she remembered many minute details about her ordeal – from her attacker's voice and appearance, to distinctive scratches on his car.

Sussex Police launched a review of the killing of Karen and Nicola in 2002, but so far no one has been charged. They must at least have considered Peter Tobin as a suspect. As we know, Tobin subjected two fourteen-year-old girls to a horrific sexual attack in 1993 in nearby Havant, and there are similarities between the two crimes.

Louise Kay

By 1988, Tobin had met his third wife, Cathy Wilson, and had fathered his second son, Daniel. That was also the year when eighteen-year-old Louise Kay disappeared in Eastbourne.

It was June, and Louise drove into Eastbourne in her dad's Ford Fiesta for a Friday night on the town with some friends, including her boyfriend. The group visited a number of bars and clubs and partied on until 4 a.m., when they decided to call it a night. Louise lived with her parents a few miles out of town, in Polegate, but she gave one of her friends a lift back to Watts Lane before heading home. Her friend jumped out of the car at around four-thirty, and Louise headed off into the night. But neither she nor the car were ever seen again.

Louise's parents had kept one of their daughter's milk teeth as a keepsake from her childhood, and it eventually enabled police scientists to compile a DNA profile for her. The profile remains on file, but no match for it has ever been found. Louise's sister, Nicola Stork, has recently been told by police that they believe Tobin was working in a hotel in Eastbourne at the time of Louise's disappearance. And he moved to Bathgate the following year, in much the same way as he would move hundreds of miles after murdering Vicky Hamilton and Angelika Kluk.

At first sight, it seems odd that the police are devoting so much time and energy to investigating possible Tobin links to crimes committed in Eastbourne and Norfolk, yet seem uninterested in those committed in the town where he lived for many years – Brighton. Perhaps there is a feeling that Tobin would not be so reckless as to murder someone on his own doorstep. But that's exactly what he did in Bathgate in 1991, when he killed Vicky Hamilton, and in 2006, when he murdered Angelika Kluk.

However, crucially, his personal circumstances were different then. At the time of Louise Kay's murder in 1988, Tobin was living with Cathy and Daniel, so bringing a victim home, with the intention of killing them, was out of the question. His attacks or abductions, if they took place, had to be conducted opportunistically, while he was out and about. As a bonus, putting some distance – even as little as twenty-five miles: the distance between Eastbourne and Brighton – between his home and a crime scene would drastically reduce the possibility of being questioned about the incident.

And who would bother asking questions of Peter Tobin anyway? As far as anyone in Brighton knew, he was simply a family man with a new-born baby.

2005 – One for the Road?

When Sussex Police learned of Tobin's frenzied knife attack on Angelika Kluk in 2006, it set alarm bells ringing with detectives investigating the murder of a thirty-five-year-old mother of three in Eastbourne in the early hours of 22 January 2005. Jennifer Kiely had gone to live in the coastal town after suffering post-natal depression, and she may have been homeless. She was stabbed sixteen times and was found dead in a beach shelter. Her killer had built and set alight a bonfire in the shelter in an attempt to destroy any evidence.

As we know, Tobin had links with Eastbourne, and he lived for many years just up the road in Brighton. However, hospital records revealed that he was being treated at the Royal Alexandra Hospital, Paisley, in the days leading up to Jennifer's murder, before being discharged on the 22nd. That would seem to rule him out of this attack, but it is hard to ignore the fact that Jennifer's murder took place just seven months after Tobin was released from his ten-year prison sentence. Furthermore, his next known attack (on Cheryl McLachlan in Paisley) did not take place until nine months later. So perhaps the hospital's records are wrong. After all, mistakes can be made, and the date given for Tobin's discharge needed to be out by only one day for him to have made it down to the south coast in time to commit the murder.

Peter Tobin has been beaten and is behind bars. This hare was finally caught by advances in DNA profiling – which allowed investigators to link him unequivocally to the deaths of Vicky Hamilton, Dinah McNicol and Angelika Kluk. However, when the police have looked further back in time, all too often they have been frustrated by the slow, steady pace of technological progress. As yet, DNA profiling has not provided any evidence to prove that Tobin murdered anybody else, although police remain hopeful that one day it will. Until then, Tobin continues to hold secrets that he may well take to the grave. He once boasted that he has killed dozens of women, but he refuses to reveal their identities. Maybe some day forensic science will do the talking for him.

What might we conclude about all of these unsolved murders and Tobin's potential relationship to them? First, we should acknowledge that we do not have access to all of Operation Anagram's files. However, when it became known that we were writing this book, a number of people contacted us and provided us with information. For example, the niece of Esther Mersey, who went missing from Port Glasgow in November 1965 in suspicious circumstances, sent us details about the case, and we forwarded them on to police contacts in Scotland. Her family has subsequently been interviewed as part of Operation Anagram, and Tobin has been eliminated as a suspect. By contrast, we have not been privy to the results of any DNA profiling that has been undertaken as part of Operation Anagram, so we cannot definitively rule out Tobin as a suspect in any of the cases that have been presented here. Nevertheless, he is a much more likely candidate in some cases than others.

We think that the best way to view these unsolved murders is in distinct groups based on geography. So we have a Norfolk Group; a South Coast Group; a Hitch-hiking Duo; and a Scottish Group. Once all of the murders have been placed in one of these four groups, Tobin can probably be ruled out as a suspect in some because of timescales – such as the Jennifer Kiely case and possibly the Jackie Ansell Lamb killing (which would mean also ruling him out of the Barbara Mayo murder, as police have established that the same man killed Jackie and Barbara) – or because there are much stronger suspects. For instance, Robert Black is far more likely to have killed Genette Tate and Suzanne Lawrence, while Russell Bishop remains the prime suspect in the 'babes in the wood' case. As for the rest, those women and girls in the Norfolk Group are most worthy of further consideration and scrutiny, while the Jessie Earl, Louise Kay, Pamela Hastie and Dorothea Meechan cases all bear some of the hallmarks of Tobin's modus operandi.

It remains to be seen whether Tobin did actually kill all or some of these women. But as Aesop's fable tells us, slow and steady eventually wins the race.

Nemo me impune lacessit

Perhaps the answer to whether Peter Tobin killed these women lies among the many items – including jewellery – discovered following his arrest. After Tobin's conviction for the murder of Dinah McNicol, the police were finally able to turn to the public for help in identifying a number of pieces of jewellery. (They had previously been unable to do so because of the risk of jeopardising the case against Tobin.) Within days, Sussex Police released several images to the press, but a spokesperson was quick to explain:

> There is no evidence or intelligence to suggest that Peter Tobin is responsible for any other crime. However, the scoping activity continues with the overall aim of establishing a timeline of Peter Tobin's movements since the 1960s. One action which is being undertaken relates to items of recovered women's jewellery which police are keen to trace and identify the owners of. These items have been traced to be in Peter Tobin's possession in 1991 and 2006. Anyone who recognises the jewellery or has information they believe will be relevant to the Operation Anagram inquiry is asked to contact their local police force.

The first three items were all British military in origin: a five-centimetre Star of the Order of the Thistle bearing the Latin motto of the Scottish regiments of the British Army – '*Nemo me impune lacessit* [No one attacks me with impunity]' – that is worn on the left breast; a cap badge from the Royal Electrical and Mechanical Engineers; and a Highlanders infantry regiment badge bearing the Gaelic motto '*Cuidich'n*

Righ [Help the King]'. Tobin had a history of burglary dating back to his adolescence, so perhaps he stole these items. But it is more likely that they were taken from his victims as trophies. Perhaps they had been given to soldiers' wives or girlfriends to wear with pride. Perhaps they were taken from Tobin's victims as they lay dead or dying.

Furthermore, could it be significant that one of the badges came from the Royal Electrical and Mechanical Engineers – the corps to which George Puttock, the husband of Bible John's third victim, belonged? Did he give that badge to his wife Helen as a keepsake? Was she wearing it on the night she was murdered by Bible John? Perhaps George, at home on leave, even insisted she should wear it before going out that night – to ward off the attentions of amorous dancing partners. Maybe Helen took it off and slipped it in her handbag before entering the Barrowland Ballroom, just as many other women removed their wedding rings or anything else that might suggest they were attached.

If all of this conjecture could be proved, it would provide a strong link between Bible John and Peter Tobin. And a number of women's rings and watches found in Tobin's possession might be equally significant. When scouring the River Cart after the murder of Pat Docker, the police found the casing from her watch, but not the watch itself. Maybe one of the wristwatches now being displayed by Sussex Police once belonged to Pat. But even if that is not the case, it seems that both Bible John and Peter Tobin were in the habit of taking watches from their victims. And it is worth pointing out that when Jessie Earl was finally found on Beachy Head, her watch was missing, too.

Among the other items of jewellery recovered after Tobin's arrest, it is striking how many of them have religious themes. There are seven religious pendants, including two St Christophers and three crosses. A small black purse embossed with the word 'Lourdes' was also found. Of course, Bible John was given his nickname by the press precisely because he seemed to be obsessed with religion, and now we know that Peter Tobin shares that obsession.

Is this a coincidence? Is it a coincidence that they both took watches from their victims? And is it a coincidence that Tobin had in his possession a military badge that may well have belonged to Bible John's third victim?

Or do they have all of these things in common because they are one and the same man?

Chapter Ten

Is Peter Tobin Bible John?

There is no such thing as chance; and what seems to us
mere accident springs from the deepest source of des-
tiny.

Friedrich Schiller, *The Death of Wallenstein* (1798)

Before attempting to answer the question that forms the title
of this chapter, we should acknowledge that we are now entering territory that has been well trodden by authors who have
written extensively not just about Bible John but about serial
killers more generally. Most obviously, a mini-industry is still
devoted to researching and speculating about the identity of
Jack the Ripper. Yet decades of research into this late-Victorian
serial killer have so far failed to identify him conclusively, in
spite of the fact that several authors have claimed the case is
now closed (as a result of their investigations). As Paul Begg,
one of the more respected 'Ripperologists', argues: 'Who was
Jack the Ripper? Who knows? I certainly don't.'

Perhaps more important to us than actually identifying Bible
John is demonstrating how we have attempted to establish

that identity, without concealing anything that was unearthed during our research. Of course, we have presented all the evidence that supports our conclusion, but we hope we have given equal consideration to anything that counters it. In short, we feel our job has been to provide all the information a reader needs to drawn their own conclusions. This is why, for example, we reproduced both the profile that we constructed and the profile draw up by Dr Brittain at the time of the murders. We have tried to show how we went about analysing the information that both of these profiles contained, and what we have learned from the secondary literature devoted to the case. In this latter respect, it is hard to escape the conclusion that much of what the world thinks it knows about Bible John has been steered in a particular direction by the first half of a nickname that was casually bestowed on him by a Glaswegian crime reporter immediately after a press conference. Moreover, that nickname was coined because of the statements given by one woman – Jeannie Williams – who was guided, controlled and perhaps even manipulated by the detective leading the investigation, Joe Beattie.

For many years, it was hoped that DNA extracted from the semen found on Helen Puttock's stocking might eventually definitively identify her killer, but we can now say that this line of enquiry is likely to prove fruitless. Detectives involved in the original investigation admit that this potentially crucial piece of evidence was probably handled and stored in such a manner in the 1960s and 1970s that by now it will be, at best, severely compromised or, at worst, worthless. As Joe Jackson says, 'I cannot see them [the stockings] being treated as gingerly as would be necessary for a clear DNA comparison.'

We are inclined to give more credence to Jackson's opinion than to that of SerialKillerCentral.com, which says, 'Cold case review DNA evidence could be on the verge of laying to rest one of the most enduring mysteries in Glasgow folklore.'

With DNA analysis unlikely ever to provide that elusive one-in-a-million match, we are obliged to look elsewhere for answers.

First, both Peter Tobin and Bible John can be classified as serial killers, as both murdered three or more people over an extended period of time. With this as the foundation, more specific comparisons have then been drawn. For example, Wikipedia states: 'There are similarities between Tobin's mugshot from that era and the photofit artist's impression of Bible John, and Tobin moved away from Glasgow in 1969, the same year that the killings officially ended.' Other websites, such as NationMonster.com, also suggest that Tobin might be Bible John, while simply typing 'Peter Tobin and Bible John' into any search engine generates more than fourteen thousand hits.

But it is not only internet bloggers who have made the link between these two killers. In a thoughtful article published by *The Times* in May 2007, Melanie Reid asks simply, 'Was Angelika's Murderer the Infamous Bible John?' She cites 'striking parallels' between Tobin's background and what is known about Bible John, and argues that it is 'credible' that Pat Docker, Mima McDonald and Helen Puttock were all killed by Tobin. Specifically, she notes that Tobin was living in Glasgow at the time of all three murders, that he was religious and known to frequent dancehalls, and that his photofit was similar to that produced in 1969. Finally, she mentions

Tobin's 'lifelong savagery towards women', a characteristic that was surely shared by Bible John.

We have learned even more about Tobin's history since he was convicted for the murders of Vicky Hamilton and Dinah McNicol, thanks to the work of Operation Anagram, the on-going investigation into his suspected other killings. Some of the information recently released by the police, when cross-referenced with evidence from the original Bible John investigations, certainly seems to point towards Tobin. In fact, some of it is so startling that to suggest it is purely coincidental would be verging on the absurd.

Jeannie Williams told the police that she and her sister shared a taxi with a man called John, which we can assume was a pseudonym. Jeannie didn't catch the surname he gave clearly, but she thought it might have been Templeton, Sempleson, or Emerson. So Helen's killer might well have identified himself as something like 'John Sempleson'. Four decades later, when police were investigating Peter Tobin's history, they soon learned that he used a variety of pseudo-nyms. In addition to the two they knew about from the Angelika Kluk murder – Pat McLaughlin and James Kelly – they found that he frequently went by the name John. Even more significantly, he often paired that with the surname Semple. John Sempleson and John Semple – what are the chances of two different serial killers adopting two such similar pseudonyms?

Tobin was also living in Glasgow when Bible John began killing. His first wife Margaret remembers visiting his parents in Paisley, a few miles to the west, and he knew his way around the city more generally. After an evening out with

Margaret before they were married, Tobin would take her back home to Earlbank Avenue, just two hundred yards from where Bible John's final victim was murdered. His pursuits at the time were solitary – he was not a team player. We said the same thing about Bible John in our profile of the killer, as did Dr Brittain in the profile he produced for Glasgow CID. The fact that Margaret cannot remember Tobin mentioning what he did during the day – he simply 'disappeared' – is likely to have been replicated in other parts of his life. He never brought friends to the flat they shared in Glasgow, probably because he didn't have any – with the exception of one: the witness at Tobin and Margaret's wedding, who may well have been living in Brighton at the time. Tobin kept himself to himself; as did Bible John, who was unknown to regulars in the Barrowland Ballroom and claimed not to be interested in either Rangers or Celtic – even though support of one or other of these clubs was an almost universal expression of team loyalty and personal identification for a Glaswegian male at the time. In a city that would become obsessed with finding Bible John, keeping yourself to yourself was a very successful strategy to avoid detection.

But was Tobin in Glasgow when the second and third Bible John murders were committed? Some websites claim that he moved away from the city after the murder of Helen Puttock, but in fact he left earlier. Margaret told us that she and Tobin were living in Brighton in 1969, and they married in the seaside town on 6 August that year, just ten days before Bible John murdered Mima McDonald in Glasgow. So might Tobin have travelled back to Scotland to commit this murder?

Unfortunately, Margaret is unable to remember Tobin's movements on precise dates over forty years ago, but she never really knew where he went when he 'disappeared', so it is certainly conceivable that he might have made the trip, and then repeated it a few months later to kill Helen Puttock. Moreover, this ties in with our assessment that Bible John was a 'commuter' – a serial killer who travelled to find suitable victims before returning to the safety of his own home. And we know from Tobin's behaviour after killing both Vicky Hamilton and Angelika Kluk that he liked to put many hundreds of miles between himself and the scene of a crime he had committed.

When drawing comparisons between Bible John and Peter Tobin, timing is crucial. There was a gap of eighteen months between Bible John's first and second murders. As we pointed out earlier, such a hiatus is consistent with the start, rather than the end, of a serial killer's killing cycle. On the other hand, the gap might have been due to the killer forming a relationship that satisfied him. During that year and a half, Tobin met, dated, lived with and married Margaret – which could easily account for the delay before Bible John struck again. Tobin could have sex whenever he wanted, he could bully, abuse and, on one occasion, almost kill, and he didn't even have to leave home to do any of these things. Put simply, his needs were satisfied by Margaret – for a time at least. But why did the Bible John killings stop at the end of 1969? It's unlikely that he grew tired of killing. Much more likely is that circumstances prevented him from doing so. Peter Tobin was arrested shortly after the third Bible John murder and spent around thirteen months in prison. Maybe Bible John didn't choose to stop killing – he was forced to call a temporary halt after being locked up.

Like Bible John, Tobin felt comfortable killing in Glasgow: he repeatedly stabbed Angelika Kluk nearly four decades later right in the centre of Bible John territory. And the manner in which Pat Docker and Helen Puttock's killer escaped (on foot and on a bus) indicates that he knew the city's western and southern suburbs well. Indeed, when we analysed Pat's murder, we came to the conclusion that her killer probably headed straight home after dumping her handbag in the River Cart. That home might have been in any one of several suburbs, but a prime candidate was Shettleston – where, at the time, Tobin and Margaret shared a flat.

What of the physical appearance of Bible John and Tobin? Are they comparable? There are no photographs of either man from 1968/9, so all we have to go on are the drawings produced by Lennox Paterson, Margaret's recollection of Tobin at the time, and more recent photographs of him. There are certainly similarities between Paterson's impressions of Bible John and photographs of Tobin (in his sixties) released after his arrest for the murder of Angelika Kluk. However, at the time of the Bible John killings – when Tobin was aged between twenty-one and twenty-three – he would obviously have looked very different from how he does now. In particular, according to Margaret, he had brown or dark brown hair, not the grey or fair hair that he has now. If Margaret remembers correctly, then that hair colour does not match the descriptions of Bible John given by the two young witnesses from the Barrowland Ballroom and Jeannie Williams. However, both men did wear their hair short, cut away from the face with slim sideburns, which was unusual for the time. We must also note the apparent discrepancy in age between Peter Tobin and witnesses' impressions of Bible John, who placed him between twenty-five and thirty-five years of age. This is, of course, a very broad age range, at its lower end not significantly more than Tobin's actual age at the time of the killings. It is also a reasonable assumption that Bible John's formal style of dress perhaps made him appear older than he actually was.

There are more issues about the two men's appearance. The three Bible John witnesses all described him as around six feet tall, whereas Tobin is significantly shorter; and none of them mentioned a scar running down the side of his left eye, which Tobin has today and had at the time. Furthermore, all three witnesses guessed Bible John was aged somewhere between twenty-five and thirty-five, while Tobin was only twenty-two at the time of Mima McDonald's murder and twenty-three when Helen Puttock was killed. These discrepancies may seem to eliminate Tobin as a suspect, but it should be remembered that the man and the woman from the Barrowland were far from confident that their descriptions of Bible John were accurate, while Jeannie Williams admitted that she had consumed a 'bucketful' of alcohol on the night her sister was murdered. Furthermore, all of them saw Bible John only in the dark, so they may well have missed the scar; and Tobin dressed unusually conservatively, so it would not be surprising if three of his peers took him for being slightly older than he really was. Finally, the behaviour of Detective Superintendent Joe Beattie needs to be mentioned. The man leading the investigation after Helen Puttock's murder may well have focused far too heavily on Jeannie's description of

Bible John while ignoring those offered by other witnesses. For example, the Barrowland's bouncers – who, in contrast to Jeannie, would probably have been sober – said that Bible John was much shorter than six feet and that he had brown or dark brown hair, not fair or reddish, as described by Jeannie. That brings the description of Bible John much closer to Margaret's recollection of Tobin at the time. So there are certainly grounds for being sceptical that the accepted image of Bible John, the one that police followed to the exclusion of all others, was accurate.

In addition, we have mentioned that some of the detectives who worked alongside Beattie felt that he held something back from them, kept something 'up his sleeve' to rule out potential suspects. None of them ever learned what this was, but is it too far-fetched to suggest that it might have been an obvious physical feature that could not be concealed – such as a scar?

That, admittedly, is conjecture, but there is no doubt about another link between Bible John and Peter Tobin – they both frequented dancehalls. Tobin met both his first and his third wife while out dancing. We also know that Margaret thought Tobin was 'totally fearless of everybody and everything – he never seemed scared'. Similar self-assurance was displayed by Bible John during the altercation with the Barrowland's manager about the cigarette machine.

There are also striking similarities between the two men's demeanour and the way they dressed. Bible John dressed distinctively for the time. He wore a well-cut, brown suit with three buttons down the front; a lapel badge; a blue shirt; what might have been a regimental tie; unfashionable suede boots, rather than shoes; and an overcoat and scarf. Tobin also liked to dress smartly, usually in jackets and ties, and often the ties were the regimental style favoured by Bible John. In fact, Tobin once told Margaret that he had been in the army.

We might interpret Bible John's argument with the Barrowland's manager and bouncers as evidence of his assumption that his opinion would be accepted – because he was confident of his superiority over others – and a reflection of his contempt for what the man represented. For Bible John, the manager was not only the formal authority figure at the dancehall, but a personification of formal authority generally – the authority of everyone who had ever exercised control over him. Bible John was not just standing up to the manager; he was standing up to his parents and all of the priests, teachers, policemen and prison officers who had impacted on his life. Similarly, Peter Tobin liked to present himself as more cultured and refined than his contemporaries, even though he never held a position of real authority. Most of his jobs involved manual labour, such as shunting, carpentry, painting and decorating, driving and café work.

Both men could be chivalrous one minute and utterly evil the next. Jeannie described Bible John as too polite for the Barrowland – he was well spoken and didn't swear – to such an extent that he stuck out like a sore thumb. He would even stand up and allow Helen to take her seat before sitting down himself. That type of chivalry was almost unheard-of at the dancehall, and it didn't end when they left. On the taxi ride home, Bible John insisted that Jeannie should be dropped off first, so she would not be left alone in the cab. However, of course, on that occasion, there was an ulterior motive behind the gallantry.

Peter Tobin displayed almost identical chivalry. He prob-ably acted like a knight in shining armour when meeting Vicky Hamilton who was waiting at the bus stop in Bathgate in 1991. And we know he played the good Samaritan when picking up Dinah McNicol later that year, soon putting the hitch-hiker (if not her male companion) at ease. And just as Helen Puttock was happy to remain in the taxi with Bible John once Jeannie was dropped off, so Dinah casually refused David Tremlett's offer to leave Tobin's car with him. These were decisions that would soon cost both women their lives.

Driving was important to Tobin, and Cathy Wilson remem-bers that he changed his car on a regular basis. The Yorkshire Ripper, Peter Sutcliffe, did the same thing – so that he could never be associated with a particular vehicle. And, of course, Tobin's mobility – his familiarity with roads, service stations and routes into and out of cities – would help him stay one step ahead of any police investigation. He could use Britain's road network to 'disappear' after committing a crime, as he did after killing Vicky Hamilton. Perhaps he did something very similar after murdering Mima McDonald and Helen Puttock – fled from Scotland to his new home on the south coast of England. Perhaps that is why Glasgow Police were unable to find Bible John.

There are also analogies between the two men's styles of killing – whom they targeted and how they killed them. All known victims of both men were strangled and sexually assaulted. Both men also used items of their victims' clothing as ligatures, gags or binds. Bible John's second and third vic-tims were strangled with their own tights or stockings. Peter Tobin used Dinah McNicol's leggings to bind her wrists and her headscarf to tie her ankles together. Years later, Cheryl McLachlan saw a tie and a belt hidden under one of the cushions of his sofa. She is convinced they would have been used to restrain and kill her, had Tobin managed to overpower her. Admittedly, none of Bible John's victims was stabbed (unlike Cheryl and Angelika Kluk), but that apparent contrast with Tobin's modus operandi can be explained by the fact that Bible John picked up his victims at a dancehall in a period of considerable gang violence, so he knew he would be searched for weapons by the Barrowland's bouncers. It would have been simply too risky for him to carry a knife. The gulf in violence exhibited by the two men in their respective attacks might also be explained by the fact that there was a gap of twenty-two years between the last Bible John murder and the first known to be committed by Peter Tobin. Bible John's ferocity increased with each victim, so it is logical to think that it would have continued to do so over the following years, if he continued to kill. By 1991, he could well have reached the level of sadistic violence that Tobin used against Vicky Hamilton and Dinah McNicol.

At first glance, there does not seem to be much correlation between the victims chosen by Bible John and those of Peter Tobin. The former targeted married women between the ages of twenty-five and thirty-two, whereas the latter's known victims ranged from just fourteen to twenty-three. However, if all of these murders *were* committed by Tobin, the apparent discrepancy can be explained quite simply by the fact that he was in his early twenties in the late 1960s, and so might well have been sexually attracted to more experienced, slightly older women, as many young men are. By the 1990s, he was a middle-aged man, and as such would hardly be alone in finding younger women irresistible. It is also worth remembering that the neighbour who found Pat Docker and the police who first arrived at the scene initially thought she was a boy. Pat was skinny, physically underdeveloped and looked younger than her true age – just the sort of appearance that Tobin favoured in the prostitutes he brought back to his home in Bathgate, twenty years later.

Religion unquestionably links these two killers. In the taxi ride he shared with Jeannie Williams and Helen Puttock, Bible John returned time and again to religious themes – 'adulterous women', praying rather than drinking on New Year's Eve, Moses, the stoning to death of a woman – which led to him being given the nickname that identifies him to this day. Meanwhile, Peter Tobin was a Catholic, and his former wives say he was well versed in religion generally and the Bible. We also know that he sought refuge with religious communities at least twice: first, with the Jesus Fellowship Church in Warwickshire, when on the run from the police in 1993; and twelve years later at St Patrick's in Anderston, prior to killing Angelika Kluk. Margaret remembers Tobin's parents' home being littered with religious iconography; and when her own mother visited the Tobins' church, the priest offered an unflattering view of Peter, which suggests that he knew him quite well. Bible John thought ill of the 'adulterous' women who attended the Barrowland's 'Over-25s' night and he described such dancehalls as 'dens of iniquity' because they encouraged married people to enjoy illicit one-night stands. Perhaps these feelings were what motivated him to kill three of these women. Perhaps, thirty-seven years later, Peter Tobin took the life of

Angelika Kluk – who was rumoured to have slept with a priest and was having an affair with a married man – out of a similarly twisted sense of moral outrage.

Also consider the items of women's jewellery discovered in Tobin's possession after his arrest, including several crucifixes, St Christophers, watches and rings. It seems certain that Tobin took these 'trophies' from his victims, in much the same way as Bible John took his victims' handbags. Intriguingly, another possible trophy in Tobin's collection was a cap badge of the Royal Electrical and Mechanical Engineers. Helen Puttock's husband was in the Royal Electrical and Mechanical Engin-eers, and he was in Glasgow on the night she died. It is eminently plausible that he gave her the badge before she went out dancing – either simply as a keepsake, or to dis-courage possible suitors. After all, what better way could there be to deflect the attentions of an over-eager dancing partner than to say that your army husband is waiting at home, and here is his cap badge to prove it?

Tobin's former wives provide a wealth of evidence about his attitude towards women – he was cruel, sadistic and sexually voracious. We also know that he continued to have sex with Margaret when she was menstruating – in her words, he would 'carry on regardless'. Indeed, she remembers that the blood made him 'more excited'. This is highly significant when we look at Bible John's 'signature'. After each murder, he left his victim's sanitary towel clearly in view – even going to the trou-ble of carefully positioning it after killing Helen Puttock. By doing this, Bible John was sending out a message that he was simultaneously disgusted and sexually aroused by these women's menstruation, just as Tobin was by Margaret's.

Tobin's vicious knife attack on Margaret, which left her vagina bleeding profusely, should be viewed in a similar light. In her moving account of that attack, Margaret says the knife became a 'metal Tampax'. Moreover, she surely would have died without the prompt action of a neighbour, so we can say with certainty that Peter Tobin was, at the very least, willing to kill in the late 1960s.

There is no evidence from the cases of Vicky Hamilton, Dinah McNicol and Angelika Kluk to indicate that Tobin was still excited by menstruation, as he had been during his marriage to Margaret. However, he may simply have deemed it wise to abandon Bible John's 'signature' in case any of his victims' bodies were ever found. More certain is that Bible John left the sanitary towels on display to signify his control over his victims' dead bodies and his disgust with women generally, and with these women in particular. And the way in which Tobin disposed of his victims' bodies indicates that he felt exactly the same way.

As Ian Brady observes, serial killers are a 'house divided': they display their 'contempt for society, yet still feel compelled to maintain their good name'. That description fits Peter Tobin perfectly, even as far back as August 1969, when Mima McDonald was killed. Earlier that month, Tobin had cemented his 'good name' by marrying Margaret, which at the time was much more socially acceptable than their previous 'living in sin' arrangement. He was always well dressed in a suit, and it should be remembered that he had wooed Margaret by acting the perfect gentleman – opening car doors for her and always getting her back to her parents' house on time after dates. The other side of this 'house divided' personality, though, involved

Tobin verbally and physically abusing Margaret, locking her indoors, and even killing her pet. Maybe it also involved him murdering Pat Docker, Mima McDonald and Helen Puttock.

To what extent does Tobin match the profile that we compiled for Bible John and the one drawn up for Glasgow Police in the 1960s? Dr Brittain suggested that the murderer would be under thirty-five years of age, introverted, withdrawn and solitary, with few close friends. He would be vain, sadistic and egocentric, and would adopt a superior manner in his dealings with other people. He would have a rich fantasy life and would be excited by weapons. His relationship with his mother would have been ambivalent – characterised by both love and hatred – while his father may have been authoritarian. Finally, Dr Brittain suggested that, even as an adult, Bible John would be something of a 'mummy's boy', and would give his mother gifts 'to a degree beyond the ordinary'. From the profile we constructed, it is interesting to note that we saw Bible John as organised and socially conservative. His conversation revealed that he saw himself as a cut above the rest. While he clearly wanted to 'have' a woman, this had to be on his own terms, because he saw women as inferior to him. They excited and appalled him in equal measure.

Much of this fits with what we know about Peter Tobin. For example, he is a sadist and is excited by weapons. He made sure that Margaret knew he carried a knife, and then indicated in the most sadistic way that he was prepared to use it on her. He had few friends and was a loner. We don't know for sure if his father was authoritarian, nor what his relationship was like with his mother. The only snippet of information we have about these two people comes from Margaret, who merely remembers them 'staring into space' when she and Tobin went to see them. However, it is interesting to speculate why Tobin took Margaret to visit his parents at all. After all, theirs was hardly a traditional courtship. Could Margaret have been 'a gift' for Tobin's mother? Was she used by Tobin to appease his family, to prove to them that he had settled down and grown up? To reinforce his self-image as a sophisticated, superior, chivalrous man about town?

Sadly, as we know, he was never any of these things at any point in his life.

Bible John and Peter Tobin: Can You Tell the Difference?

The young man in his twenties stood in front of the mirror, ran his hand over his short hair and tightened the knot of his tie. Only once he was satisfied he was smart enough did he leave by the front door. He walked with a certain confidence, as he knew these streets well. He'd lived in Glasgow most of his life. But as he passed people along the street, he knew no one would recognise him, because no one really knew him. Even those he called friends. He preferred it that way. Fewer ties made it easier to move around. He could disappear at a moment's notice and didn't need to tell anyone where he was going. Tonight, to ensure his anonymity, he'd also use a fake name – John Sempleson.

It was a Thursday evening, and just like everyone else he was heading out in search of nightlife. But unlike those he'd meet that evening, his search for excitement would not be driven by alcohol or dancing. His thrill would be achieved by trapping his young female victim. Tonight he would kill.

For him, women served one purpose – sex. He wanted it when it suited him and he liked it rough. If they put up a struggle, he would hurt them. Some of the women he'd meet tonight would almost certainly be in relationships or married. He knew he was better than them, and it pained him to visit the venues they frequented. But they had to be tolerated because they were where his prey congregated, and he could move about unnoticed among the throngs of people.

It had been a while since he'd last killed. His personal circumstances had made it impossible. But he was confident that he still knew exactly what to do. Confident that he would find a victim, too. A man of such culture and sophistication as himself would act like a magnet to the type of woman he was after. She would be slim and would have shoulder-length dark hair. If she looked younger than the 'Over-25s' policy at the dancehall dictated, all the better. He would turn on the charm and be the perfect gentleman. They would find him endearing and would quickly be lulled into feeling relaxed around him. Others might view him as over-familiar, but he was only concerned about one person's opinion, and she would see him as a harmless flirt. He had plenty of money – cash in hand most of the time, because of the nature of the work (both legitimate and otherwise) he did – so he'd buy every round. Plying his victim with alcohol meant they would find it harder to fight back later. Then, at the end of the night, he would complete his final chivalrous act and see the lassie home – or rather *almost* home. If any other passengers had come along for the ride, he would ensure they were dropped off first, allowing him to be alone with his victim. Finally, once the time was right, when there were no witnesses around, he would sadistically attack his unsuspecting victim.

If the alcohol had worn off, he would subdue her first with a beating before strangling her to death. He liked to use items of clothing worn by his victims – tights or stockings could be used to strangle or bind. Of course, an important part of the attack would be sexual – he didn't mind how he got it, but it had to be rough, and if the woman was injured in the process that would excite him even more. His attacks had become increasingly violent since he began, and he now knew that he was aroused by blood. Once his victim was motionless, he would take something that belonged to her. Jewellery, perhaps, something they wore to attract men. It disgusted him that women wore crosses or St Christophers and yet carried on in such an indecent way – especially the married ones.

Afterwards, he would lie low, perhaps get out of town altogether, to put some distance between himself and the police.

He smiled, suspecting that they might one day catch up with him. He might even let them, once he'd had enough.

With that, he caught a glimpse of his latest victim, walked over and introduced himself. 'Nice to meet you. I'm John.'

He didn't know how the night would end. But that was part of the thrill.

It is impossible for us to *prove* that Peter Tobin is Bible John. But, throughout the process of writing this book, as our research intensified and our knowledge of Tobin and Bible John developed, we have gradually become certain that Tobin is indeed this notorious Glasgow serial killer. We accept that there are still difficulties in making this assertion, but this seems to us inevitable with cases dating back to the 1960s. So too the element of time also helps to explain a lack of consistency in some of the case-specific materials that we have presented about a number of murders. The idea that offenders would be consistent in how they commit murder over several decades is in reality far-fetched, and so we should not be too worried that offenders change what they do and how they do it as they grow older and more experienced.

It is perhaps worth reiterating here our main reasons for coming to the conclusion that Peter Tobin *is* Bible John. Tobin is a convicted, commuting serial killer that we now know was living in Glasgow, or travelling to and from the city, at the time of the Bible John murders. We also know a great deal about his behaviour at the time of these murders through his then partner – Margaret Mackintosh. The picture that emerges about Tobin in the late 1960s fits Bible John perfectly, even if there are some discrepancies in relation to some of the contemporary physical descriptions that were provided and which have become part of the Bible John story. However, what is not in doubt is the psychological and structural picture of Tobin's behaviour, especially his behaviour towards women. Tobin was suave and charming when he needed to be, and a dominating sexual sadist when he was alone with a woman. He is an almost perfect example of what Ian Brady called a 'house divided'. Even as late as 2005, Tobin was considered by Cheryl McLachlan to be a 'kindly old gent'. It was of course this very charm that allowed him to gain access to his victims.

Added to this structural picture of Peter Tobin as Bible John is a myriad of other Bible John connections: Bible John's conversations in the Glasgow taxi and then many years later Tobin's conversation when he picked up David Tremlett and Dinah McNicol; the jewellery that was found in Tobin's possession after his arrest, which just so happened to include a REME cap badge – which is of course the regiment that Helen Puttock's husband belonged to; his frequent use of Glasgow hospitals (and nor should we forget that Pat Docker – Bible John's first victim – was a nurse in the city); Tobin's knowledge of the Glasgow streets; his fondness for dancehalls; his religious background and his regular use of aliases.

Finally, there is the question of Bible John escaping justice. This had been one of the biggest manhunts in Scottish police history, with literally thousands of man hours devoted to the case. The police became so desperate that they even resorted to using a medium. Even so, Bible John evaded justice. How are we to explain this failure? Did Bible John simply stop murdering, or perhaps he was arrested for some other crime and his imprisonment prevented him for killing again? Perhaps he died. Of course another explanation might be that Bible John was an organised, commuting serial killer who was travelling back and forth across the country after he had killed in Glasgow. In an age before DNA profiling and a national DNA database, this would be an ideal way to keep one step ahead of the police. We cannot be certain that Tobin understood all of this in the late 1960s, but whether by design, or perhaps simply through luck, he did manage to escape justice in Glasgow by travelling south to Brighton. Thankfully, that luck eventually ran out with the murder of Angelika Kluk and, as far as we are concerned, the organised, commuting serial killer that murdered Pat Docker, Jemima MacDonald and Helen Puttock *was* Peter Tobin.

Bible John? Case closed.

A Guide to Further Reading

Mini-publishing industries have been devoted to both the great city of Glasgow and its most notorious son – Bible John. Space precludes us from mentioning all of these books, so we shall list only those works that we believe will help readers with their own research, and those that may provide insights into how we formed our conclusions. Allan Massie's (1989) *Glasgow – A History* (London: Barrie & Jenkins), Bruce Durie's (2000) *A Century of Glasgow* (Stroud: Sutton), David Daiches's (1977) *Glasgow* (London: André Deutsch) and Peter Reed's (1999) *Glasgow: The Forming of the City* (Edinburgh: Edinburgh University Press) were of particular use in providing background detail on Glasgow. Meanwhile, Alan Spence's (1977) *Its Colours They Were Fine* (London: Collins) and Archie Hind's (1966) *The Dear Green Place* (Edinburgh: Birlinn) were two works of fiction that gave us a strong sense of the atmosphere in the city in the 1960s. Of particular help in understanding Glaswegian policing in that decade was Joe Jackson's (2008) *Chasing Killers: Three Decades of Cracking Crime in the UK's Murder Capital* (Edinburgh: Mainstream). We also used Les Brown and Robert Jeffrey's (2005) *Glasgow Crimefighter: The Les Brown Story* (Edinburgh: Black & White), although we relied on this less than Jackson's account. Both Jackson and Brown – two detectives who were working in Glasgow in the 1960s – describe the Bible John investigation in detail, and each has his own opinion about how the inquiry was handled. Brown goes as far as to identify someone he believes is Bible John – a suspect he arrested at the time who gave his name as John White. However, as we discuss in the text, this man has since been correctly identified and eliminated as a suspect.

We make extensive use of James Patrick's (1973) *A Glasgow Gang Observed* (London: Eyre Methuen), which was based on field research undertaken by Patrick and is a rich source of ethnographic detail about gang members' clothes, music, dancing and attitudes towards violence, gender and sex. Many other books also deal with crime in Glasgow, such as Reg McKay's (2006), *Murder Capital: Life and Death on the Streets of Glasgow* (Edinburgh: Black & White) and, most recently, Douglas Skelton's (2009) *Glasgow's Black Heart: A City's Life of Crime* (Edinburgh: Mainstream), which discusses the links between Peter Tobin and Bible John. It is only fair to point out here that Skelton is sceptical that Tobin and Bible John are one and the same man: 'I know of one academic who is busy as I write trying to link Tobin to the Bible John killings . . . there is a danger that we might elevate an insignificant little pervert into the answer to a great mystery' (pp. 302–3). We presume that Skelton is referring to this book, and respectfully disagree with his opinion. Aside from anything else, whether Tobin is Bible John or not, he *is* a convicted serial killer, so it is hard to dismiss him as 'an insignificant little pervert'.

Numerous books deal with the Bible John killings, although many of them are sensationalist. However, we found Alan Crow and Peter Samson's (1998) *Bible John: Hunt for a Serial*

Killer (Glasgow: First Press) and Charles Stoddart's (1980) *Bible John: Search for a Sadist* (Edinburgh: Paul Harris) bucked the trend. Stoddart's book is especially useful. It is carefully argued and therefore much more reliable than most books devoted to this subject, and much of it is based on extensive interviews with Joe Beattie, the detective in charge of the investigation, who died in 2000. We relied heavily on Stoddart to build up a picture of the Bible John murders. Of note, he also helpfully reproduces Dr Robert Brittain's (1970) paper 'The Sadistic Murderer' as an appendix.

We refer in the text to David Leslie's (2007) *Bible John's Secret Daughter: Murder, Drugs and a Mother's Secret Heartbreak* (Edinburgh: Mainstream), which tells the story of Hannah Martin. And we consulted Geoffrey Garrett and Andrew Nott's (2001) *Cause of Death: Memoirs of a Home Office Pathologist* (London: Robinson) to gain an insight into how pathologists worked in the 1960s. More generally in this area, we referred to Keith Simpson's (1980) *Forty Years of Murder* (London: Grafton) and Colin Evans's (2007) *The Father of Forensics: The Groundbreaking Cases of Sir Bernard Spilsbury, and the Beginnings of Modern CSI* (Cambridge: Icon). For details about the psychic Gerard Croiset, we consulted the largely credulous Jack Pollack's (1964) *Croiset the Clairvoyant* (New York: Doubleday) and counterbalanced that with the more sceptical Alan J. Whiticker's (2006) *Searching for the Beaumont Children: Australia's Most Famous Unsolved Mystery* (Milton: John Wiley & Sons Australia).

We consulted a variety of academic sources to explore the topic of serial killing. David Wilson's (2009) *A History of British Serial Killing* (London: Sphere) can be used to put the Bible

John murders into historical context, and it allows Peter Tobin's killing cycle to be compared with those of other mass murderers. Similar themes are explored in David Wilson's (2007) *Serial Killers: Hunting Britons and Their Victims, 1960–2006* (Winchester: Waterside Press), while a more populist approach can be found in David Wilson and Paul Harrison's (2008) *Hunting Evil: Inside the Ipswich Serial Murders* (London: Sphere). This latter book contains a wealth of detail about DNA profiling and the role it played in the conviction of Steve Wright.

Fiona Brookman's (2005) *Understanding Homicide* (London: Sage) has quickly established itself as the standard introduction to the investigation of murder, and it provides readers with plenty of background detail on the development of the police's *Murder Investigation Manual*. Another impressive book on this subject is S. D'Cruze, S. Walklate and S. Pegg's (2006) *Murder* (Cullompton: Willan). Readers might also like to consult the FBI's crime classification manual, edited by J. E. Douglas, A. W. Burgess, A. G. Burgess and R. K. Ressler (1997): *Crime Classification Manual: A Standard System for Investigating and Classifying Violent Crimes* (New York: Simon & Schuster). A good introduction to offender profiling remains Peter Ainsworth's (2001) *Offender Profiling and Crime Analysis* (Cullompton: Willan).

At the heart of profiling is the premise that the characteristics of an offender can be deduced from a carefully considered examination of the offence. In particular, the crime scene is regarded as reflecting the murderer's behaviour and personality. So analysis of how the crime was committed, why the victim was chosen, etc. can tell us what type of person the offender is. This concept presumes that an offender will always behave in the same way, regardless of context. A good, critical examination of this idea can be found in Laurence Alison's (ed.) (2005) *The Forensic Psychologist's Casebook: Psychological Profiling and Criminal Investigation* (Cullompton: Willan), which also introduces the reader to a more psychological approach to profiling and suggests how psychologists might help with police investigations.

Within the text, we refer to geographically transient serial killers, specifically Robert Black and Peter Sutcliffe. Their cases are outlined within the aforementioned *A History of British Serial Killing*, but readers might also like to consult Ray Wyre and Tim Tate's (1995) *The Murder of Childhood: Inside the Mind of One of Britain's Most Notorious Child Murderers* (Harmondsworth: Penguin), which provides a wealth of detail about the murders committed by Black. For more detailed analysis of Sutcliffe, see Michael Bilton's (2003) *Wicked beyond Belief: The Hunt for the Yorkshire Ripper* (London: HarperCollins) and Gordon Burn's (1984) *Somebody's Husband, Somebody's Son: The Story of Peter Sutcliffe* (revised and reprinted, London: Faber & Faber, 2004). Lawrence Byford's (1981) *The Yorkshire Ripper Case: Review of the Police Investigation of the Case – Report to the Secretary of State for the Home Office* (London: Home Office) was made public as a result of a Freedom of Information request in June 2006 (and therefore after Bilton and Burn had published their accounts of the case). It can be downloaded from the Home Office website at www.homeoffice.gov.uk. We also highlight the research into 'geographic profiling' undertaken by the forensic psychologist Professor David Canter. His (2003) *Mapping Murder: Walking in Killers' Footsteps* (London: Virgin) is probably the best place to start in gaining an understanding of his theories.

A number of 'true crime' books provided rich detail on several serial killers. These include Brian Masters's (1986) *Killing for Company: The Case of Dennis Nilsen* (London: Coronet), a classic of the genre, largely because Masters interviewed Nilsen and had access to his writing; Paul Begg's (2006) *Jack the Ripper: The Facts* (London: Robson); and Carole Peters's (2005) *Harold Shipman: Mind Set on Murder* (London: Carlton), one of the better 'true crime' accounts of the Shipman case. For a more academic perspective on Shipman, see K. Soothill and D. Wilson's (2005) 'Theorising the Puzzle that is Harold Shipman', *Journal of Forensic Psychiatry and Psychology*, Vol. 16 No. 4, pp. 658–98.

Finally, with a great deal of circumspection, we consulted Ian Brady's (2001) *The Gates of Janus: Serial Killing and Its Analysis by the 'Moors Murderer'* (Los Angeles: Feral House). This book is difficult to find in Britain and, as can be imagined, it is a rather self-serving affair. Brady rarely gives away anything about his own mindset – preferring to generalise about other mass murderers, especially Sutcliffe – but his concept that a serial killer is 'a house divided' remains useful.

Acknowledgements

David Wilson would like to thank a number of people who helped immeasurably in the completion of this book. Judi Martin read several draft chapters and suggested a number of helpful changes, and former Detective Superintendent Joe Jackson – who as a young detective worked on the Bible John case – was very generous with his time and also read several chapters relating to Glasgow and the Bible John investigation. I would also like to thank Charles Lavery formerly of the *Sunday Mail*, Reevel Alderson of BBC Scotland and the staff and librarians of Birmingham City University, Cambridge University and the Radzinovich Institute of Criminology at Cambridge University. Detective Inspector Alan Webster of the West Midlands Police and Nick Howe – formerly of Staffordshire Police but now at the Centre of Applied Criminology at Birmingham City University – were also helpful through their willingness to discuss murder investigations. Of note, Morag Fyfe, Senior Search Room Archivist at the National Archives of Scotland, answered a number of queries about Glasgow Sheriff Court records from the 1960s and 1970s. The noted Scottish lawyer John Ward kindly discussed a number of cases with me and Naomi Faulkner at Birmingham City University kindly kept track of

264   THE LOST BRITISH SERIAL KILLER

our various drafts. At Curtis Brown, Gordon Wise again skilfully guided the book from proposal to completion with grace and good humour, and Jacquie Drewe, Adam Banham and Renay Richardson were as usual helpful and often far too indulgent – especially on a Thursday. At Sphere, Antonia Hodgson, Hannah Boursnell and Kirsteen Astor were at all times encouraging and kind, and Antonia in particular has gone out of her way to make writing this book a pleasurable and fulfilling experience.

Paul Harrison would also like to thank those who have supported and helped him write *The Lost British Serial Killer*. As ever, John Ryley, Head of Sky News, and Simon Cole, Managing Editor, have afforded invaluable access to Sky's television and online content concerning all cases involving Peter Tobin. To that end, Ben Veasey in the VT library worked to help find some of the more compelling images of the cases of Angelika Kluk, Vicky Hamilton and Dinah McNicol as they unfolded. And in the Sky stills library, Andreas Kirchberger helped immeasurably in locating key images of those involved in these tragic stories, as he did for *Hunting Evil*. I would also like to thank Five News Crime Correspondent Jason Farrell and Producer Neal Mann who traced and interviewed Peter Tobin's ex-wife Sylvia Jefferies. Indeed, thanks to all three of Peter Tobin's former wives, including Cathy Wilson and Margaret Mackintosh, who suffered so much at the hands of an evil man, yet were so brave in telling their haunting stories. Gordon Wise at Curtis Brown has, as ever, been the voice of reason throughout. And echoing Prof Wilson's words on all those at Sphere – including Antonia Hodgson, Hannah Boursnell and Kirsteen Astor – your support and guidance must surely be unrivalled. Finally, my family, and my wife Felicity in particular, never waiver in their encouragement, even at 2 o'clock in the morning. Thank you.

Index